best | designed

Martin Nicholas Kunz . Hanna Martin

honeymoon hotels

avedition

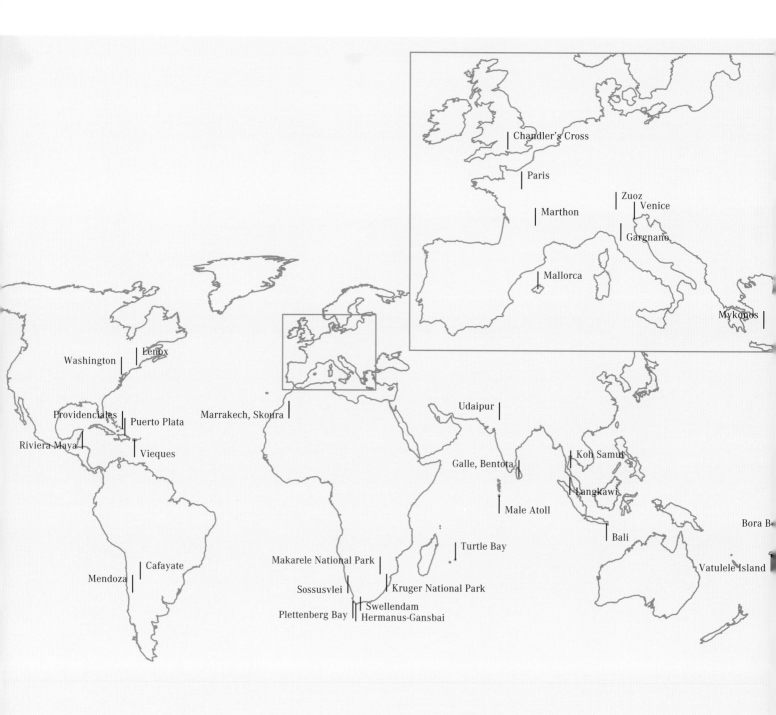

Chandler's Cross

Paris

Zuoz

Venice

Marthon

Gargnano

Mallorca

Mykonos

Lenox

Washington

Providenciales

Puerto Plata

Marrakech, Skoura

Udaipur

Koh Samui

Riviera Maya

Vieques

Galle, Bentota

Langkawi

Male Atoll

Bali

Bora B

Turtle Bay

Cafayate

Makarele National Park

Vatulele Island

Mendoza

Sossusvlei

Kruger National Park

Swellendam

Plettenberg Bay

Hermanus-Gansbai

01 02

One of the oldest definitions of the term 'honey-moon' originates from English essayist Samuel Johnson (1709-1784) and is at the same time also one of the most beautiful: "Honeymoon is the first month after marriage, when there is nothing but tenderness and pleasure." A whole month full of affection—which however in Johnson's time most couples spent within their own four walls; nowadays it sweeps them away to the most hidden corners of the world. Honeymoon has become a synonym for a "once in a lifetime" journey, for an unforget-

table vacation, which should be romantic and sensual, emotional and unique like no other.

It begins with the selection of the destination: many newlyweds jet straight off from the altar to tropical islands—right at the top of the list are the Maldives, Mauritius and the Seychelles or the Fiji islands—to lie on white beaches, feel the warm breeze on their skin and to watch sunsets that even Hollywood directors could not stage more impressively: to find their very own personal paradise. And in the contemporary Garden of

Eden of course they don't want to stay under trees or palms, but in seafront suites, beach bungalows or overwater villas. in hideaways, which offer total privacy, indulge all senses and surprise with the service, from the morning bath of flowers to the evening candlelight dinner; everything that just married couples desire.

The expectations of paradise are high—but the snakes there, are unfortunately not so rare; for many a dream wedding voyage has turned into a nightmare due to false pretences or false

03 04

promises. But honeymoon hotels, which have the potential to be heaven on earth, do exist. This book presents some of them—on islands and at different locations around the globe; with a focus on aesthetic architecture and elaborate design. They could be historical buildings, which harmoniously fit in to a cityscape and revive the splendor of bygone times, or new resorts, which are built in perfect unity with nature. There are classical interiors, where the antiques tell a story, and puristic designs, defined by clear lines. And not to forgot the highlights, that add the finishing touches to a hotel—like the fragrant products in the bathroom, the coordinated choice of art-works or the spectacular pool layout. All of these hotels create the perfect setting, where the substance of a honeymoon trip really comes into its own, and where the honeymoon becomes what it should be: the first month after marriage, when there is nothing but tenderness and pleasure.

01 | Mayflower Inn & Spa

02 | Casa Colonial

03 | Singita Sweni Lodge

04 | Tsala Treetop Lodge

Eine der ältesten Definitionen des Begriffs Honeymoon stammt vom englischen Essayisten Samuel Johnson (1709-1784), und ist zugleich eine der schönsten: „Der 'Honeymoon' ist der erste Monat nach der Hochzeit, in dem es nichts anderes als Zärtlichkeit und Vergnügen gibt." Ein ganzer Monat voller Liebkosung und Genuss – zu Johnsons Zeiten verbrachten ihn die meisten Paare noch in den eigenen vier Wänden, heute zieht es sie in die versteckten Winkel der Welt. Honeymoon ist zum Synonym für eine Reise der Kategorie „Einmal im Leben" geworden, für einen unvergesslichen Urlaub,

der so romantisch und sinnlich, so emotional und einzigartig sein soll wie kein zweiter.

Das beginnt schon bei der Auswahl des Ziels: Viele frisch Verheiratete jetten direkt vom Altar auf tropische Inseln – ganz oben auf der Rangliste stehen die Malediven, Mauritius und die Seychellen oder die Fiji-Inseln – um an weißen Stränden zu liegen, die warme Brise auf der Haut zu spüren und in den Sonnenuntergang zu blicken, den selbst Hollywood-Regisseure nicht stimmungsvoller inszenieren könnten. Kurz: um ihr ganz persönliches Paradies zu finden. Und

natürlich möchten sie im zeitgemäßen Garten Eden nicht mehr unter Bäumen oder Palmen wohnen, sondern in Seafront-Suiten, Beach-Bungalows oder Overwater-Villas. In Refugien also, die Privatsphäre pur bieten, alle Sinne verwöhnen und vom morgendlichen Blumenbad bis zum abendlichen Candlelight-Dinner mit allem Service überraschen, den man sich just married wünscht.

Die Erwartungen ans Paradies sind hoch – und die Schlangen dort leider gar nicht so selten; schon manche Hochzeits-Traumreise ist aufgrund übertriebener Vorstellungen oder falscher

07 08

Versprechungen zum Alptraum geworden. Doch es gibt Honeymoon Hotels, die das Potenzial zum Himmel auf Erden haben. Dieses Buch stellt einige von ihnen vor – auf Inseln und an anderen Orten rund um den Globus; mit dem Schwerpunkt auf ästhetischer Architektur und durchdachtem Design. Das können historische Gebäude sein, die sich harmonisch in ein Stadtbild einfügen und den Glanz vergangener Zeiten wieder aufleben lassen oder neue Resorts, die in vollkommener Einheit mit der Natur gebaut wurden. Es gibt klassische Interieurs, deren Antiquitäten Geschichten erzählen, und puristische

Designs, die von klaren Linien bestimmt werden. Und nicht zu vergessen die Highlights, die einem Hotel den letzten Schliff verleihen: die duftende Pflegeserie im Bad, die geschickte Auswahl der Kunstwerke oder der sensationell angelegte Pool. All diese Häuser schaffen einen perfekten Rahmen, in dem die Details einer Hochzeitsreise erst richtig zur Geltung kommen und der Honeymoon das wird, was er sein soll: „…der erste Monat nach der Hochzeit, in dem es nichts anderes als Zärtlichkeit und Vergnügen gibt."

the grove | chandler's cross . united kingdom

DESIGN: Fox Linton, Fitzroy Robinson

40 minutes by car north-west of London you will find this hotel still in family possession. The castle-like stately home dates from the 18th century and is located in the middle of an approximately 300 acres typically English park. Once it harbored such illustrious guests as Queen Victoria or Edward VII. Even today it still exudes an atmosphere of the old stately country life. It combines the luxurious ambience of a manor-house with the forms, colors and materials of nature. And thus offers the traditional country house atmosphere for the city elite who want a breath of fresh air. In contrast to the traditional exterior, the interior is furnished with chandeliers, art objects, extravagant materials, and fixtures adorned with genuine Swarovski crystals. Natural colors, white patent leather furniture, and plexiglas elements, as well as wood from indigenous green oak are found in the rooms as stylistic elements. Those who prefer luxury and opulence will feel right at home in the Victorian-style rooms with their rich velvet coverings, black ostrich feathers, and dark patent leather furniture. The Sequoia Spa in an old riding stable is a special attraction with the rare privilege of an ESPA ayurveda treatment; it promises to raise guests to another level of consciousness.

40 Autominuten nordwestlich von London findet man dieses, sich noch in Familienbesitz befindende Hotel. Das schlossartige Anwesen aus dem 18. Jahrhundert liegt inmitten einer rund 120 Hektar großen typisch englischen Parklandschaft. Einst beherbergte es so illustre Gäste wie Königin Viktoria oder Edward VII. Auch heute noch strahlt es die Atmosphäre alten herrschaftlichen Landlebens aus. Es vereint auf gelungene Weise das Luxus-Ambiente eines Herrenhauses mit den Formen, Farben und Materialien der Natur. Das Hotel bietet traditionelle Landhausatmosphäre für eine städtische Elite, die Landluft atmen möchte. Im Unterschied zum repräsentativen Äußeren sind die Innenräume mit Kronleuchtern, Kunstobjekten, extravaganten Stoffen und mit Swarovski-Kristallen verzierten Einrichtungsgegenständen ausgestattet. Natürliche Farben, weiße Lackmöbel und Plexiglaselemente sowie Holz aus heimischer Grüneiche sind als stilistische Elemente in den Zimmern zu finden. Wer es luxuriös und opulent liebt, wird sich in den Zimmern im viktorianischen Stil mit schweren Samtbezügen, schwarzen Straußenfedern und dunklen Lackmöbeln wohlfühlen. Das Sequoia Spa in einem alten Stallgebäude lockt mit dem seltenen Privileg einer ESPA Ayurveda-Behandlung; sie verspricht, die Gäste auf eine höhere Bewusstseinsebene zu heben.

01 | Traditional elegance combined with contemporary design.
Zeitgenössisches Design gepaart mit edlen Materialien.

02 | Sleep like Queen Victoria—large beds, high ceilings and sound-absorbing textiles make it possible.

Schlafen wie Queen Victoria – große Betten, hohe Räume und schalldämpfende Textilien machen es möglich.

03 | The Sequoia Spa, named the most extraordinary wellness oasis in Great Britain 2005.

Das Sequoia Spa – 2005 zur außergewöhnlichsten Wellness-Oase Großbritanniens gekürt.

04 | 300 acres of park and garden surround the over 200 year-old manor house.

120 Hektar Park und Gärten umgeben das über 200 Jahre alte Herrenhaus.

chateau de la couronne | marthon . france

DESIGN: Mark Selwood, Nicky Cooper

The south-west of France is tailor-made for honeymoons: unlike the classic tourist regions such as Brittany, Provence or the Côte d'Azur masses of people don't vacation here, the hotels are not heavily overbooked and the restaurants not hopelessly overpriced. Here where the Dordogne and Charente departments meet, one can enjoy the real French "art de vivre" in idyllic landscapes—and especially, since the existence of Chateau de la Couronne. British television presenter and designer Mark Selwood has transformed the little 16th century picture book castle into an elegant boutique hotel with style, charm and sophistication. Five en-suite rooms have completely different designs—but they do have some things in common such as luxurious furnishings and views over the hotel's own park. The azure blue pool allures in the middle of the countryside—and one can relax even more wonderfully in the castle lounges, which glisten with a noble mixture of furniture, accessories and artworks. Incidentally, many pieces can be purchased—which solves the problem of finding the perfect, stylish wedding gift for your partner.

Der Südwesten Frankreichs ist für Flitterwochen wie geschaffen: Im Gegensatz zu klassischen Ferienregionen wie der Bretagne, der Provence oder der Côte d'Azur verbringen hier keine Menschenmassen ihren Urlaub, die Hotels sind nicht chronisch ausgebucht und die Restaurants nicht hoffnungslos überteuert. Dort, wo sich die Departements Dordogne und Charente treffen, kann man in idyllischer Landschaft echtes französisches „savoir vivre" genießen – besonders, seit es das Chateau de la Couronne gibt. Der britische Fernsehmoderator und Designer Mark Selwood hat das Bilderbuchschlösschen aus dem 16. Jahrhundert in ein elegantes Boutiquehotel mit Stil, Charme und Raffinesse verwandelt. Fünf en-suite-Zimmer zeigen sich in völlig unterschiedlichen Designs. Allen gemeinsam sind die luxuriöse Ausstattung und der Ausblick über den hauseigenen Park. Mitten im Grünen lockt auch der azurblaue Pool – fast noch schöner entspannt man aber in den Schloss-Lounges, die mit einer edlen Mischung aus Möbeln, Accessoires und Kunstwerken glänzen. Viele Stücke können übrigens gekauft werden, womit sich die Frage nach dem perfekten Hochzeitsgeschenk für den Partner wie von selbst und sehr stilsicher erledigt.

01 | A castle, straight out of a picture book.

Ein Schloss wie aus dem Bilderbuch.

02 | The five suites are all designed individually and offer chic luxury
and gorgeous bathrooms.

Die fünf Suiten sind alle unterschiedlich designt und bieten edlen
Luxus sowie traumhafte Bäder.

03 | After its meticulous renovation, the castle combines old structure
with modern design.

Nach sorgsamer Renovierung verbindet das Schloss alte
Bausubstanz und modernes Design.

04   05

06

04 | Sculptures, furniture and artworks can even be purchased by the guests.

Viele Skulpturen, Möbel und Kunstwerke können sogar käuflich erworben werden.

05 | The castle lounges are popular and cozy meeting points in the heart of the house.

Die Schloss-Lounges sind beliebte und gemütliche Treffpunkte im Herz des Hauses.

06 | Even on the staircase traditional style meets contemporary design.

Sogar im Treppenhaus trifft traditioneller Stil auf zeitgemäße Accessoires.

01 | The nobility of materials are in the foreground.

Die Noblesse des Materials steht im Vordergrund.

bourg tibourg | paris . france
DESIGN: Jaques Garcia

There is a small, yet extraordinary hotel in the heart of the Marais district, one of the picturesque quarters of the French capitol. The hotel with its 30 beds stands on a street of houses built in close proximity to each other and a number of charming boutiques and restaurants. It is an excellent starting point for a walk to Paris' noted sites of art and culture, for example: the Centre Pompidou, Nôtre Dame church, the Picasso Museum, the Place des Vosges and many more. The interior designer, Jaques Garcia, creatively focused on a historicized décor during the complete renovation of the hotel. The result is a fabulous mixture of various styles ranging from the end of the 19th century. You will find rooms in the Fin-de-Siècle style with the typical elements of orientalism. However, what is most apparent is the ever-present harmony of materials, colors and light compositions. The cozy inner courtyard created by Camille Muller is an artistic jewel and, on top of everything, is an oasis in the middle of the bustling metropolis.

Im Herzen des Stadtteils Marais, ein pittoreskes Viertel der französischen Hauptstadt, liegt das kleine außergewöhnliche Hotel. Das 30-Betten-Haus liegt in einem Straßenzug mit eng aneinandergedrängten Häusern und einer Vielzahl von charmanten Boutiquen und Restaurants. Es eignet sich hervorragend als Ausgangspunkt für Spaziergänge zum Centre Pompidou, Nôtre Dame, dem Picasso-Museum, dem Place des Vosges und vielen anderen Kunst- und Kulturstätten. Der Innenarchitekt Jaques Garcia hat bei einer Komplettrenovierung den gestalterischen Schwerpunkt auf eine historisierende Ausstattung gelegt. Resultat ist eine gelungene romantische Melange verschiedener Stilrichtungen vom Ende des 19. Jahrhunderts. So findet man etwa Zimmer im Stil des Fin de Siècle mit den dafür typischen Elementen des Orientalismus. Ins Auge fällt dabei immer die Harmonie von Material, Farbe und Lichtkomposition. Auch der kleine lauschige Innengarten, gestaltet von Camille Muller, ist ein gestalterisches Kleinod und obendrein eine Oase inmitten der geschäftigen Großstadt.

02 | A relaxing element in a hectic city—a small, green oasis.

Beruhigendes Element in einer hektischen Großstadt – eine kleine grüne Oase.

03 | Designs according to historical paradigms.

Entwürfe nach historischem Vorbild.

04 | Every room is thoroughly composed to the very last detail.

Jeder Raum ist durchkomponiert bis ins Detail.

05 | The bathroom—more than just a place of personal hygiene.

Das Bad - mehr als nur ein Ort für die Körperpflege.

hotel castell | zuoz . switzerland

DESIGN: Ben van Berkel, UN Studio; Hans-Jörg Ruch, Architektur Büro Ruch

The view is of tracks for cross-country skiing, the Zuoz-Madulain golf course in the summer and the Engadine Mountains stretching out in front of it all. The Castell is enthroned over the valley, and has the most beautiful panorama. The hotel, which was built in 1912 reopened in 2004 after renovation and is numbered among the new highlights of the Engadine mountain valley and in one leap has made it into the top 20 list of vacation hotels. An entire team of architects and artists have shaped the design. The conversion was carried out by UN Studio Amsterdam (Chesa Chastlatsch, Hamam, half of the rooms). The other half of the rooms was planned by architecture office Ruch from St.Moritz. An additional dash of color was injected by architect Gabrielle Hächler and artist Pipilotti Rist in 1998 with their "Red Bar" and by Tadashi Kawamata with his delicate sun terrace. They drew on regional, tradition-bound structures and local materials and solid handicrafts. Even in the selection of materials they limited themselves to raw cement and iron, glass, one kind of wood and one kind of stone. The 66 guest rooms also bear the signature of the planners: excitement, contrasts and minimalism. The rock pool, a wading pool, surrounded by a wooden platform, and a small Finnish sauna, both under the open sky, ensure your relaxation and well-being. A complement to this are massages and other treatments in the Hamam. Awaiting guests in the historic restaurant or at lunchtime on the wooden terrace is fresh, imaginative cuisine; a mixture of brasserie-style and a dash of Asia.

In Sichtdistanz Loipen, im Sommer der Golfplatz Zuoz-Madulain und davor breitet sich das Engadin aus. In schönster Aussichtslage thront das Castell über dem Tal. Das 1912 erbaute und 2004 mit Erweiterungen wieder eröffnete Hotel zählt zu den neuen Höhepunkten des Engadins und schaffte es auf Anhieb unter die Top 20 der Ferienhotels. Ein ganzes Team aus Architekten und Künstlern prägte die Gestaltung. Der Umbau stammt vom UN Studio Amsterdam (Chesa Chastlatsch, Hamam und die Hälfte der Zimmer), die andere Häfte der Zimmer plante das Architektur Büro Ruch aus St. Moritz. Einen zusätzlichen Farbtupfer setzten die Architektin Gabrielle Hächler und die Künstlerin Pipilotti Rist im Jahre 1998 mit ihrer „Roten Bar" sowie Tadashi Kawamata mit der filigranen Sonnenterrasse. Sie griffen auf regionale, traditionsgebundene Bauformen zurück und bedienten sich regionaler Materialien und solidem Handwerk. Schon bei der Wahl der Werkstoffe beschränkten sie sich auf rohen Beton und Stahl, Glas, eine Holz- und eine Steinart. Auch in den 66 Gästezimmern zeigt sich die Handschrift der Planer: Spannung, Gegensätze und Reduktion. Für Entspannung und Wohlbefinden sorgen das Felsenbad, ein Plantschpool, umgeben von einer Holzplattform und eine kleine finnische Sauna, beides unter freiem Himmel. Eine Ergänzung dazu sind Massagen und andere Behandlungen im Hamam. Im historischen Restaurant oder mittags auf der Holzterrasse erwartet den Gast eine frische, ideenreiche Küche, eine Mischung aus Brasserie und einem Schuss Asien.

01 | The view of the Engadine mountains is fascinating.

Faszinierend ist der Blick auf die Bergwelt des Engadins.

02 | 03 | 04 Rooms from the original days are combined with modern architecture.

Räume aus der Gründerzeit verbinden sich mit moderner Architektur.

04

01 | Tobacco brown and creme white—the color scheme of the house.

Tabakbraun und Cremeweiß – die Farben des Hauses.

charming house dd.724 | venice . italy

DESIGN: Mauro Mazzolini

Just a stone's throw from the Guggenheim Museum and near to Canal Grande there is the hotel Charming House DD.724. There is no real mystery behind this abbreviation: it is simply the address, Dorsoduro 724. Following the complete redevelopment and remodeling of the Palazzo, that originates prior to the beginning of the 18th century, a hotel was constructed here that is diametrically opposed to the tourist clichés of the souvenir-type Venice. It is a prime example of elaborate renovation and remodeling. The limited spatial factors of the Palazzo were allowed for through reduction. Even the smallest rooms and hallways could be optically enlarged for spacious views and perspectives using a minimalist interior decor in wood and leather, a refined light design, and by restricting the color scheme to only tobacco brown and creme white. Every room was planned to the minute detail and stands for a perfect combination of maximal comfort, the most modern house and communication technology, and holistic design. Small details, for example, old ceiling beams remind us of the former substance of the house. The view from the window falls directly into the garden of the Guggenheim Museum. The hotel with its seven rooms and suites is the ideal location for those interested in culture and lovers of a romantic short holiday.

Nur einen Steinwurf vom Guggenheim Museum entfernt und in der Nähe des Canal Grande findet sich das Hotel Charming House DD.724. Hinter der Abkürzung verbirgt sich nichts anderes als seine Adresse: Dorsoduro 724. Nach der kompletten Sanierung und Umgestaltung des Palazzos, der vom Beginn des 18. Jahrhunderts stammt, entstand dort ein Hotel, das den touristischen Klischeevorstellungen von einem Souvenir-Venedig diametral gegenübersteht. Es ist ein Paradebeispiel für eine durchdachte Renovierung und Umgestaltung. Den begrenzten räumlichen Gegebenheiten des Palazzos wurde durch Reduktion Rechnung getragen. Mit einer minimalistischen Innenausstattung in Holz und Leder, raffiniertem Lichtdesign und der Beschränkung auf die Farben Tabakbraun und Cremeweiß konnte selbst in schmalsten Räumen und Gängen optisch noch Platz geschaffen werden für großzügige Durchblicke und Perspektiven. Jedes Zimmer wurde bis ins Detail geplant und steht für eine perfekte Verbindung von maximalem Komfort, modernster Haus- und Kommunikationstechnologie und ganzheitlichem Design. Kleine Details wie etwa alte Deckenbalken erinnern an die Substanz des Hauses. Der Blick aus dem Fenster fällt direkt auf den Garten des Guggenheim Museums. Das Hotel mit nur sieben Zimmern und Suiten ist der ideale Standort für Kulturinteressierte und Liebhaber eines romantischen Kurzurlaubs.

| The artistic design of the rooms is manifest.

Die künstlerische Ausgestaltung der Zimmer ist Programm.

| The breakfast room–interesting perspectives through optimum room layout.

Der Frühstücksraum - interessante Perspektiven durch optimale Raumaufteilung.

grand hotel a villa feltrinelli | gargnano . italy

DESIGN: Pamela Babey

It's as if time has stood still in this small spot by Lake Garda. Just like a film setting, right on the west bank, is the Villa Feltrinelli, which was built in 1892. The former summer residence of the industrialist and publisher Feltrinelli dynasty was returned to its original condition under strict monumental preservation requirements and opened up as a luxury hotel in 2001. Upon entering the hall of the small neo-Gothic castle, a journey begins into the time of grand balls, pomp and glory. The skylight and the many windows, some in the shape of stars, flood the room with an exclusive light. The floor-to-ceiling frescoes reach the sky painted full of angels. An ambience of elegance and understatement. This consistent style also continues in the 21 rooms and suites. Heavy fabrics, dark woods, marble walls and antique furniture dominate the rooms. Luxurious, spacious bathrooms round off the perfect picture. An exquisite restaurant, a library, a large pool made of natural stone and its own harbor, sum up everything that is special and unique about the Grand Hotel. In the well-tended park of the villa is the guesthouse La Limonaia, where the lemon trees bear fruit.

Es scheint, als sei die Zeit in diesem kleinen Ort am Gardasee stehen geblieben. Wie in einer Filmkulisse, direkt am Westufer, liegt die 1892 erbaute Villa Feltrinelli. Der ehemalige Sommersitz der Industriellen- und Verlegerdynastie Feltrinelli wurde unter strengen Denkmalschutzauflagen wieder in ihren Originalzustand gebracht und 2001 als Luxushotel eröffnet. Betritt man die Halle des kleinen neogotischen Schlosses, beginnt eine Reise in die Zeit von großen Bällen, von Prunk und Gloria. Das Oberlicht und die vielen Fenster, einige in Sternform, fluten den Raum mit einem vornehmem Licht. Die Fresken reichen vom Boden bis zur Decke und enden in einem gemalten Himmel voller Engel. Ein Ambiente von Eleganz und Exklusivität. Dieser konsequente Stil setzt sich auch in den 21 Zimmern und Suiten fort. Schwere Stoffe, dunkle Hölzer, Wände aus Marmor und antikes Mobiliar beherrschen die Räume. Luxuriöse, geräumige Bäder runden das perfekte Bild ab. Ein exquisites Restaurant, eine Bibliothek, ein großer aus Natursteinen gemauerter Pool und ein eigener Hafen machen das Besondere und Einmalige des Grand Hotels aus. Im gepflegten Park der Villa steht das Gästehaus La Limonaia, in der Zitronenbäume Früchte tragen.

01 | Here the guest is king and can wallow in stylish luxury.

Hier wird der Gast zum König und kann in stilvollem Luxus schwelgen.

Noble, large bathrooms are reminiscent of times gone by.

Edle, große Badegemächer erinnern an alte Zeiten.

The parquet flooring in the suites is decorated with intarsia and the walls are adorned with ornaments.

Die Parkettböden in den Suiten sind mit Intarsien und die Wände mit Ornamenten verziert.

A place that has inspired artists and cast a spell on great statesmen.

Ein Ort, der schon Künstler inspirierte und große Staatsmänner in seinen Bann zog.

son brull hotel & spa | mallorca . spain
DESIGN: Ignazi Forteza

In 2003 in the ruins of an old monastery, the origins of which go far back into the 18th century, a modern luxury hotel was opened after careful restoration. The Son Brull Hotel & Spa is situated in the north of Majorca, among olive groves and remote from the hectic hustle and bustle of the cities. The owner family has succeeded in preserving the historic architecture and masterfully combining it with modern interiors. For the new design they commissioned young, local designer Ignazi Forteza. He didn't only prove his sensitivity to atmosphere and well-being, but he also took into consideration the typical attitude towards life on the island. And so from outside the state still looks like a Majorcan country house but inside the guests find state-of-the-art design. All 23 rooms and suites are decorated in gentle, harmonious natural colors and equipped with high-tech. This appreciation of detail is also evident in the spa. As the first wellness oasis on the island, only regional products like sea salt, rosemary, honey, olive and almond oils are used. Guests come to spend their time in Son Brull mainly because of the serenity and clarity of the house. One can relax by the pool, read a book in a quiet corner and look forward to the evening meal in the fine restaurant "365".

In den Gemäuern eines alten Klosters, dessen Ursprünge weit in das 18. Jahrhundert zurückreichen, wurde 2003 nach sorgfältiger Restaurierung ein modernes Luxushotel eröffnet. Das Son Brull Hotel & Spa liegt im Norden von Mallorca, inmitten von Olivenhainen und fern vom hektischen Treiben der Städte. Der Eigentümerfamilie ist es bei dem Objekt gelungen, historische Architektur zu bewahren und gekonnt mit modernem Interieur zu verbinden. Für die Neugestaltung beauftragte sie den jungen einheimischen Designer Ignazi Forteza. Er bewies nicht nur Feingefühl für Atmosphäre und Wohlbefinden, sondern berücksichtigte das typische Lebensgefühl der Insel. So wirkt das Anwesen von außen nach wie vor wie ein mallorquinisches Landhaus. Doch im Inneren finden die Gäste neustes Design: Alle 23 Zimmer und Suiten sind in sanften, harmonischen Naturfarben gehalten und mit Hightech ausgestattet. Sinn fürs Detail beweist auch das Spa. Bei der ersten Wellness-Oase auf der Insel kommen nur regionale Produkte wie Meersalz, Rosmarin, Honig, Oliven- und Mandelöle zum Einsatz. Wer im Son Brull seine Zeit verbringt, kommt vor allem wegen der Ruhe und der Übersichtlichkeit des Hauses. Man entspannt sich am Pool, liest in einer stillen Ecke ein Buch und freut sich auf die feinen Abendessen im Restaurant „365".

01 | The signature of the architect is unmistakable, who together with the owners has paid attention to every last detail, both inside and out. Big, white king size loungers under awnings invite you to relax.

Unverkennbar ist die Handschrift des Architekten, der zusammen mit den Eigentümern auf jedes Detail geachtet hat, innen wie außen. Große weiße Kingsize-Liegen laden unter Sonnensegeln zum Entspannen ein.

02 | The pool and park-like garden are the ideal setting for sunset parties.

Pool und parkartiger Garten bilden den idealen Rahmen für Partys bei Sonnenuntergang.

03 | The stately finca is located near to Pollença in the North of the island.

Die herrschaftliche Finca liegt nahe Pollença im Norden der Insel.

04 05

06

04 | The designers have kept decorative features to an absolute minimum in all of the 23 rooms.

Bei den 23 Zimmern haben die Designer auf jeglichen Dekorations-ballast verzichtet.

05 | The restored olive press in the u-bar tells the agricultural stories of the finca.

Die restaurierte Olivenpresse in der u-bar zeugt von der landwirtschaftlichen Geschichte der Finca.

06 | The historical charm of the façade and the minimalist interior design are only separated by the door to the lobby.

Die historische Anmut der Fassade und die minimalistische Innenarchitektur sind nur durch die Türschwelle zur Lobby getrennt.

ostraco suites | mykonos . greece

DESIGN: Zannis Konkas, Aggelos Aggelopoulos, Dimitrios Mantikas

Idyll, luxury, and the beauty of nature—the hotel offers this mixture on the Greek island of Mykonos. The complex sits high on a throne on the hill top near the center of the city of Mykonos, allowing a view of the sea of white houses and the blue of the Aegean Sea. The architecture harmoniously combines the tradition of the Greek island with the modern. Romantic corners are unified with an accentuated, modern style. The color white dominates the formation. The natural stone walls are whitewashed and are found in the interior as well as the exterior. A particular emphasis was placed on harmony when selecting the decor: of course, you will find all the modern comforts in the hotel, but also traditional furniture and many textiles in earthy tones define the picture. Terraces and inner courtyards make the hotel a place to relax and create seamless transitions from the rooms to the open areas in nature. A pleasing unison of old and new, of retreat and Mediterranean vitality, of sense of taste and informal charm creates atmosphere of the hotel.

Idylle, Luxus und die Schönheit der Natur – diese Mischung bietet das Hotel auf der griechischen Insel Mykonos. Die Anlage thront auf einer Bergkuppe in der Nähe des Zentrums von Mykonos-Stadt mit einem Ausblick über das weiße Häusermeer und das Blau des Ägäischen Meeres. Die Architektur verbindet auf harmonische Weise die Tradition einer griechischen Insel mit der Moderne. Es vereinen sich romantische Winkel mit einem betont jungen Stil. Bei der Errichtung dominiert die Farbe Weiß in der auch die Natursteinwände, die sich sowohl in den Innen- als auch den Außenräumen wiederfinden, getüncht sind. Bei der Ausstattung wurde viel Wert auf Harmonie gelegt: Es finden sich moderne Annehmlichkeiten im Haus, traditionelle Möbel und viele Textilien in Erdtönen bestimmen das Bild. Terrassen und Innenhöfe machen das Hotel zu einem Ort der Entspannung und schaffen nahtlose Übergänge von den Zimmern und öffentlichen Räumen zur Natur. Ein wohltuender Einklang von Alt und Neu, von Rückzug und mediterraner Lebendigkeit, von Sinn für Geschmack und familiärem Charme prägt die Atmosphäre des Hauses.

02 | Chic dreams in blue and white.

Schicke Träume in Blau und Weiß.

40 | ostraco suites

03 | Two wedding chapels are part of the hotel complex.
Zwei Hochzeits-Kapellen gehören zur Anlage.

04 | The pool with the suite ensures a little refresher.
Der Pool in der Suite sorgt für Erfrischung.

dar ahlam | skoura . morocco

DESIGN: Thierry Teyssier

Shaped out of clay and baked by the sun, protective and proud the castle homes of the Berbers soar in the high valley of the Dadès in the south Moroccan desert. From such a Kasbah in the oasis of Skoura, with lots of sophistication French entrepreneur Thierry Teyssier, created the Dar Ahlam, his "house of dreams". He has established a very creatively styled luxury hotel, where oriental living traditions are combined with French "savoir vivre" and modern comforts. Rounded arches, ornamental folding screens, patios and water basins, as well as the masterful use of light and shade embody the Arabian language of shape. The five acre large garden with date palms and scarlet red bougainvillea is a lush, fragrant oasis within an oasis. Reflected in the water of the T-shaped swimming pool are the square towers of the castle, and from the terrace you can look out over the snow-capped summit of the High Atlas Mountains. The spa offers ranges from the traditional Hamam to outdoor massages, which are given in Bedouin tents. Also belonging to the Kasbah are three individual villas, which can be rented. Not only honeymooners, can make the sensual dreams of 1001 Nights come true.

Aus Lehm geformt und von der Sonne gebacken, wehrhaft und stolz ragen die Wohnburgen der Berber im Hochtal des Dadès aus der südmarokkanischen Wüste. Aus einer solchen Kasbah in der Oase Skoura hat der französische Unternehmer Thierry Teyssier mit viel Raffinesse das Dar Ahlam, sein „Haus der Träume" geschaffen. Entstanden ist eine kreativ gestylte Luxusherberge, in der sich orientalische Wohntraditionen mit französischem „savoir vivre" und modernem Komfort verbinden. Rundbögen, mit Ornamenten durchbrochene Paravents, Patios und Wasserbecken sowie der gekonnte Umgang mit Licht und Schatten verkörpern die arabische Formensprache. Der zwei Hektar große Garten mit Dattelpalmen und scharlachroten Bougainvillea präsentiert sich als eine üppige, duftende Oase in der Oase. Im Wasser des T-förmigen Swimmingpools spiegeln sich die quadratischen Türme der Burg, und von der Terrasse blickt man auf die schneebedeckten Gipfel des Hohen Atlas. Das Wellness-Angebot reicht vom traditionellen Hamam bis zu den Outdoor-Massagen, die in Beduinenzelten verabreicht werden. Zur Kasbah gehören auch drei einzeln zu mietende Villen, die nicht nur für Hochzeitspaare ein Ambiente schaffen, in dem sich die sinnlichsten Träume von 1001 Nacht erfüllen können.

01 | The castle hotel of Dar Ahlam towers in the oasis of Skoura, not far from Marrakech.

Die Hotelburg Dar Ahlam erhebt sich in der Oase Skoura unweit von Marrakesch.

02 | Local craftsmen and artists created the interior decoration.

Lokale Handwerker und Künstler kreierten die Inneneinrichtung.

03 | Oriental nights: sleeping under a canopy.

Orientalische Nächte: schlafen unter einem Baldachin.

04 | Find your inner peace over a mint tea by the spa pool.

Zur inneren Ruhe findet man beim Minztee am Spa-Pool.

02

03

04

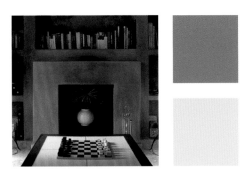

casa lalla | marrakech . morocco
DESIGN: Annabel and Pierre Olivier

It offers space for private moments and for lively conversations. It also has its own restaurant and hamam. Casa Lalla is such a riad in which all the rooms are situated around a central inner courtyard . Thus Arabian architecture meets the demands of visitors from all over the world. Even if their wedding party does not fill all three suites and five rooms, they still may reserve the entire hotel for themselves. This ensures the most privacy possible. In addition, there is also an all-inclusive service which includes transfer from the airport, tours through Marrakech, and massages in the hamam. The design is a combination of Western standards mixed with Arabic tradition. Mosaics, bricked archways, and ornate wrought iron lattices inspire, just as with the numerous lanterns, dreams from 1001 Arabian Nights. Thanks to the combination of neutral colors ranging from sand to stone and very simple furniture, the decor never seems overpowering. After all, it is a basic element of Moroccan hospitality to allow the guests to rest and give them room to allow their own personality to develop.

Er bietet Raum für private Momente und für anregende Gespräche. Für das leibliche Wohl sorgen ein eigenes Restaurant und ein Hamam. Das Casa Lalla ist ein solcher Riad, in dem sämtliche Zimmer um einen zentralen Innenhof angeordnet sind. Dabei erfüllt die arabische Architektur die Ansprüche von Besuchern aus aller Welt. Auch wenn sie mit ihrer Hochzeitsgesellschaft nicht alle der drei Suiten und fünf Zimmer belegen, können sie das Haus komplett für sich reservieren. Das sichert die größtmögliche Privatsphäre. Im Angebot ist außerdem ein besonderer All-Inclusive-Service, der den Transfer vom Flughafen, Stadtführungen durch Marrakesch und Massagen im Hammam umfasst. In punkto Design verschmelzen westliche Standards mit arabischer Tradition. Mosaike, gemauerte Torbögen und verschnörkelte schmiedeeiserne Gitter wecken, genau wie zahlreiche Laternen, Träume aus 1001 Nacht. Dank der Kombination mit gedeckten Farben von Sand bis Stein und sehr geradlinigem Mobiliar wirkt die Innenausstattung aber niemals überladen. Schließlich gehört es zu den Grundsätzen marokkanischer Gastfreundschaft, dem Gast Ruhe zu gönnen und ihm Raum für Entfaltung der eigenen Persönlichkeit zu geben.

01 | The Perle d'Ambre suite with its own fireplace is among the most beautiful in the hotel.

Die Suite Perle d'Ambre mit eigenem Kamin gehört zu den schönsten des Hauses.

02 | The guests will find the decorative Arabian archways in the halls and in their rooms.

Die geschwungenen arabischen Torbögen findet der Gast in den Gängen und auf seinem Zimmer.

03 | The cozy, open inner courtyard is the central meeting place.

Der gemütliche offene Innenhof ist der zentrale Treffpunkt.

the oberoi, mauritius | turtle bay . mauritius

DESIGN: Lek Bunnag, H. L. Lim

When most people think of Mauritius the two blue and orange famous stamps, highly sought-after among collectors, spring to mind. However, the island is less well known as a tropical destination or as the perfect place for those longing to travel to far-off places. This new resort opens up the opportunity to discover a fascinating country, beyond its volcano stone and rich vegetation, surrounded by coral reefs. The villas are embedded within abundant natural beauty. Sophisticated luxury is the philosophy of the renowned Indian hotel group, which with their "spin-off" has topped the already excellent hotel industry of the island. Guests experience a blend of different continents and cultures in the design of the villas. The infinity pool is surrounded by columns like a ruin. You may be reminded of Africa in the spa. A bath filled with flowers has a Far East feel to it. The villas with their own pool and garden keep with the zeitgeist and offer great comfort with traditional furniture setting the course. But at the end of the day it is the calm and inner contemplation, which singles out this resort. It is aimed at couples who want to enjoy an extensive spa program and seek a joint experience of wellbeing and peace of mind.

Bei Mauritius denken wohl die meisten an jene zwei berühmten Briefmarken, die blaue und rote, hoch begehrt unter Sammlern. Weniger im Blick: Der Inselstaat als tropische Destination für Fernwehgeplagte. Dabei liegt Mauritius nur unweit der Seychellen, besitzt durch den Vulkanstein eine reiche Vegetation und ist fast ganz von Korallenriffen umgeben. Die Villen sind in eine faszinierende Landschaft eingebettet. Raffinierter Luxus ist das Credo der renommierten indischen Hotelgruppe, die mit ihrem Ableger der ohnehin schon ausgezeichneten Hotellerie auf der Insel noch eins oben drauf gesetzt hat. Im Design der Villen und Angebote erleben die Gäste eine Mischung verschiedener Kontinente und Kulturen. Der Infinity-Pool ist umstellt mit Säulen wie eine antike Ruine. Im Spa mag man sich an Afrika erinnert fühlen. Ein mit Blüten gefülltes Bad mutet fernöstlich an. Die Villen entsprechen indes dem Zeitgeist und bieten hohen Komfort, einige haben ihren eigenen Pool und Garten. Traditionelle Möbel setzen die Akzente. Am Ende aber sind es die Ruhe und innere Einkehr, die dieses Resort herausheben. Ideal für Paare, die sich mit einem reichen Spa-Programm gut und glücklich miteinander fühlen wollen.

01 | One of the garden villas with its own pool. Volcano stone on the ground ensures a natural appearance.

Eine der Gartenvillen mit eigenem Pool. Vulkanstein als Boden sorgt für ein natürliches Aussehen.

02 03

02 | The furniture comes from different cultures.

Die Möbel entstammen verschiedenen Kulturen.

03 | The British influences of the crown colony are reflected in the living design.

Britische Einflüsse auf die Kronkolonie spiegeln sich im Wohndesign wider.

04 | Among the original style elements are rock architecture and palm roofs.

Zu den ursprünglichen Stilelementen gehören Felsarchitektur und Palmendächer.

04

05

01 | Even when the resort is fully occupied with a maximum of 22 guests you'll still feel like it's just the two of you in the bush villas.

Selbst bei voller Belegung mit maximal 22 Gästen ist in den Buschvillen Zweisamkeit gewährleistet.

little kulala | soussusvlei . namibia

DESIGN: Laurie Owen, Andy Chase

Steppes, mountains and dried out riverbeds—this is the Namibian desert. In the middle of this landscape is the Little Kulala. It can be found on 52 acres of private land and borders the "Namib Naukluft Park". The estate offers an impressive view over the famous sand dunes of "Sossusvlei" and of large mountain landscapes and open expanses. Eight chalets provide accommodation in Little Kulala. Every house has its own bathroom with shower. All buildings stand on wooden platforms, which ensure good air circulation. Guests can even spend the night under the open skies on the roof. Here you can watch the stars with your partner, or alone. In the main house of the lodge are the bar, dining area, the lounge and a small pool. A nearby waterhole means that you can observe animals like bat-eared foxes or jackals quenching their thirst. A variety of activities is also on offer, for example an exploration trip in the desert, looking at rock drawings or going on a ride in a hot air balloon.

Steppen, Berge und ausgetrocknete Flussbetten – das ist die namibische Wüste. Inmitten dieser Landschaft befindet sich das Little Kulala. Sie liegt auf einem 21.000 Hektar großen Privatgelände und grenzt an den „Namib Naukluft Park" an. Die Anlage bietet einen eindrucksvollen Blick auf die berühmten Sanddünen von „Sossusvlei" sowie auf großartige Berglandschaften und offene Ebenen. Als Unterkunft stehen im Little Kulala acht Chalets zur Verfügung. Jedes Haus verfügt über ein eigenes Badezimmer mit Dusche. Alle Gebäude stehen auf Holzplattformen, die für eine gute Luftzirkulation sorgen. Die Gäste können sogar auf dem Dach unter freiem Himmel übernachten. Hier kann man in Ruhe mit seinem Partner oder auch alleine den Sternenhimmel betrachten. Im Haupthaus der Lodge sind Bar, Speisebereich, Lounge und ein kleiner Pool zu finden. Ein nahes Wasserloch bietet die Möglichkeit, Tiere wie Löffelhunde oder Schakale dabei zu beobachten, wie sie ihren Durst löschen. Außerdem wird eine Vielzahl von Aktivitäten angeboten, wie zum Beispiel Erkundungsfahrten in die Wüste, Ausfahrten zu den einheimischen Felszeichnungen oder Ballonfahrten.

02 | From the terrace the view stretches away into the land.

Von der Terrasse geht der Blick weit hinein ins Land.

03 | In a canopied bed in the middle of the desert. The chalets also provide shade.

Im Himmelbett mitten in der Wüste: Die Chalets spenden auch Schatten.

04 | Residents do not have to go without bathroom comforts in their rooms.

Auf Badekomfort müssen die Bewohner in ihren Zimmern nicht verzichten.

05 | Earth and natural colors dominate the furniture, flooring and walls.

Erd- und Naturfarben dominieren das Mobiliar, die Böden und Wände.

03 04

05

01 | The style of houses: open construction and natural materials.

Der Stil der Häuser: offene Bauweise und natürliche Materialien.

singita sweni lodge | kruger national park . south africa

DESIGN: Boyd Ferguson, Cecile and Boyd; Andrew Makin, OM Design Workshop

Crocodiles look down their long noses out of the water. Off the sides, baboons swing through a tree. On a pallet under a tree, you are lying on your belly, being massaged by four hands at the same time. A snapshot that gives an impression of life at this lodge. It belongs to an ensemble of four destinations of the Lebombo Concession that lies directly on the Sweni River on the eastern border of the Krueger National Park. Built on four posts, here a main house with restaurant and spa, as well as six extremely spacious suites, await the guests. A small but refined camp for people who also want to escape the hectic on the safari. The rooms have a mostly open structure—a picture window to the wilderness. They sit high above the nearby river like eagles' nests. The pale wood of the supports and the posts make them seem like huts. However, the ambiance is made more elegant through its interior made of glass, slate, leather, and steel. The African accessories, rattan furniture, pottery made of clay or masks and animal hides highlight this modern and sophisticated style. The lodge is an exclusive hideaway that allows lazy days as well as tours through the national park or active care for body and soul.

Krokodile schauen mit ihren langen Mäulern abwartend aus dem Wasser. Abseits turnen Paviane in einem Baum. Man selbst liegt bäuchlings auf der Pritsche unter einem Baum und wird gleich von vier Händen massiert. Ein Schnappschuss, der einen Eindruck gibt vom Leben in dieser Lodge. Sie gehört zu einem Ensemble von vier Destinationen der Lebombo Konzession, direkt am Fluss Sweni am östlichen Rand des Krüger Nationalparks gelegen. Auf Pfählen errichtet warten hier ein Haupthaus mit Restaurant und Spa sowie sechs ausgesprochen geräumige Suiten auf die Gäste. Ein überschaubares Lager für Menschen, die dem Trubel auch auf Safari entfliehen wollen. Die Räume sind großteils offen gestaltet – ein Schaufenster in die Wildnis. Wie Adlerhorste thronen sie über dem nahen Fluss. Das bleiche Holz des Gestänges und Pfähle lassen sie wie Hütten anmuten. Doch mit dem Interieur aus Glas, Schiefer, Leder und Stahl veredelt sich das Ambiente. Auch die afrikanischen Accessoires, Möbel aus Korbgeflecht, Krüge aus Ton oder Masken und Felle, pointieren diesen modernen und anspruchsvollen Stil. Die Lodge versteht sich als ein exklusiver Hideaway, der träge Tage genauso ermöglicht wie Touren durch den Wildpark oder die aktive Pflege von Körper und Seele.

03 | Furniture and decor made of rattan and clay are African, tables
and sideboards have a Western influence.

Möbel und Dekor aus Korb und Ton sind afrikanisch, Tische und
Sideboard westlich geprägt.

04 | The open construction of the loft suites is also the same for the rooms.

Die offene Konstruktion der Loft-Suiten wurde auch für die Zimmer übernommen.

royal malewane | greater kruger area . south africa

DESIGN: Ralph Krall, Phil and Liz Biden

Africa does extraordinary things to your soul and Royal Malewane is an advance on the senses. It is here that you find the perfect balance of nature's wild pulse and the quiet sophistication of comfort, elegance and style. The eight suites, linked by wooden walkways and each with its own wooden deck, gazebo and private plunge pool, are completely surrounded by the untamed Africa bush. The Royal and Malewane suites offer a private kitchen, dining area and private game drives. The "Big Five" of the wilderness are found here in the heart of South Africa: lion, leopard, elephant, buffalo and rhinoceros. At night, leave the richly-decorated shutters on the windows open, and let the wild night sounds lull you to sleep, but do not be surprised to hear the bone-chilling roar of a lion! Game viewing is a thrill in open vehicles or on foot, with the expert rangers and trackers. Royal Malewane has the only working Master Tracker in Southern Africa. After the pleasure of the world-class cuisine, why not enhance the feeling and indulge in a spa treatment with a traditional African theme, while you drift off to the distant sounds of animals readying themselves for another night's hunt.

Afrika wirkt sich auf außergewöhnliche Weise auf die Seele aus und das Royal Malewane ist ein Paradies für die Sinne. Hier findet man die perfekte Mischung aus pulsierender Wildnis und ruhiger Beschaulichkeit mit Komfort, Eleganz und Stil. Die acht durch Holzstege verbundenen Suiten besitzen jeweils ein eigenes mit Gazebo überdachtes Holzdeck sowie einen privaten Pool, an den auf allen Seiten der ungezähmte afrikanische Busch angrenzt. Die Suiten des Royal Malewane bieten eine eigene Küche, einen Essbereich und zudem private Safari-Trips. Hier im Herzen Südafrikas findet man auch die „Big Five" der Wildnis: Löwe, Leopard, Elefant, Büffel und Nashorn. Nachts sollte man die reich verzierten Fensterläden offen lassen und sich von den Klängen der Wildnis in den Schlaf wiegen lassen. Es kann jedoch durchaus passieren, dass man durch das Gebrüll eines Löwen wieder aufgeschreckt wird! Das Beobachten von Wildtieren ist am spannendsten in Begleitung eines Wildhüters und Rangers im offenen Fahrzeug oder zu Fuß. Royal Malewane verfügt über den einzigen noch tätigen Master Tracker in ganz Südafrika. Nach dem Genuss der Spitzen-Cuisine kann man das Wohlbefinden durch eine traditionelle, afrikanische Wellness-Behandlung noch steigern, während man sich von den fernen Rufen nachtjagender Raubtiere davontreiben lässt.

01 | Even the king-sized canopy bed underwent a long trip before it became part of the royal ambiance.

Auch das Kingsize-Himmelbett hatte bereits eine weite Reise hinter sich, als es Teil dieses herrschaftlichen Ambientes wurde.

02 | Watch the animals drink at the spa pool, whilst having an A[...] treatment.

Während einer afrikanischen Wellness-Behandlung kann m[...] Tiere beim Trinken am Pool beobachten.

03 | **04** There are only eight suites in this luxurious camp, in th[...] middle of the wilderness, each with its own pool.

In diesem Luxuscamp inmitten der Wildnis gibt es nur acht Suiten, jede mit eigenem Pool.

05 | Feel like a king in the Victorian baths, with soft, upholstered chaise longues.

Leben wie ein König – in den viktorianischen Bädern mit de[...] weich gepolsterten Chaiselongues.

03 04

05

01 | A tower-like room houses the lodge's library.

Ein turmartiges Zimmer beherbergt die Bibliothek der Lodge.

marataba | marakele national park . south africa

DESIGN: Jill Hunter, Jacqui Hunter, Nicholas Plewman & Hunter Family

The Waterberg Mountains in the north of South Africa have always fascinated people. Nowadays this region is a national park, where you can go game viewing, and not just for the famous "Big Five". This is where the Marataba Lodge has set up its camp. It opened in 2006 and is looking to bridge the gap between innovative luxury and the experience of African culture and wilderness. Its architecture reflects the nearby ruins of "Great Zimbabwe"—a city steeped in legend in the south of the neighboring state. And so the house is made of unveiled brickwork. It gives the reception, restaurant and lounge of the lodge a homey, almost quaint ambience. The counterpart to the dominant quarrystone is formed by taut awnings. They bring a camping feeling into the nature. Like a tent they span the roof of the 15 suites in the bush. Inside a fabric canopy wafts above the heads of the guests. Under this they sleep in king size beds, surrounded by weapons and other old cultural artifacts. The bathroom is open plan and a thick-walled bathtub made of stone takes center stage. And this can all be found within the environment of the wilderness, which also has its attractions—that can be well observed from the veranda of the suite. Or you can get even closer: and soak it in with all senses during a nighttime excursion with park guides.

Die Waterberge im Norden von Südafrika faszinierten schon immer die Menschen. Heute ist diese Region ein Nationalpark, in dem man auf die Pirsch gehen kann, nicht nur nach den berühmten „Big Five". Hier hat die Lodge Marataba ihr Lager aufgeschlagen. Sie eröffnete 2006 und sucht den Brückenschlag zwischen innovativem Luxus und dem Erleben von afrikanischer Kultur und Wildnis. Ihre Architektur reflektiert die nahen Ruinen von „Great Zimbabwe", eine von Sagen umrankte Stadt im Süden des Nachbarstaates. So besteht das Haupthaus aus frei liegendem Mauerwerk. Es verleiht Rezeption, Restaurant und Lounge der Lodge ein anheimelndes, fast altertümliches Ambiente. Den Gegenpart zum dominanten Bruchstein bilden gespannte Planen. Sie stimmen auf ein Camping-Leben im Freien ein. Wie ein Zelt überspannen sie das Dach der 15 Suiten im Buschland. Innen schwebt ein Stoffhimmel über den Köpfen der Gäste. Darunter schlafen sie in Kingsize-Betten, umgeben von Waffen und anderen alten Kulturgegenständen. Das Bad ist offen zum Raum und rückt eine dickwandige Badewannenschale aus Stein in den Mittelpunkt. Das alles mutet anspruchsvoll an im Umfeld der Wildnis. Doch auch die setzt ihre Reize – gut zu beobachten von der Veranda der Suiten. Oder eben noch näher dran: mit allen Sinnen aufzusaugen bei nächtlichen Exkursionen mit Parkguides.

02

02 | The tented suites are distributed throughout the bush.

Die Zelt-Suiten verteilen sich im Buschland.

03 | Light effects highlight the comfortable sleeping place and the open bathroom.

Lichteffekte fokussieren den komfortablen Schlafplatz und das offene Bad.

04 | Boma is the name of the open fire, where you can eat outside at night.

Boma heißt das offene Feuer, an dem man nachts draußen speist.

05 | The brick-work is made of quarrystones, which come from the rocks of the Waterberg Mountains.

Das Mauerwerk besteht aus Bruchsteinen, die von den Felsen der Waterberge stammen.

03 04

05

01 | Clear lines and colorful design at the foot of the Langeberg Mountains.

Klare Linien und farbenfrohes Design am Fuß der Langeberg
Mountains.

bloomestate | swellendam . south africa

DESIGN: Joke Hensema

Swellendam, halfway between Cape Town and the Garden Route, is the third oldest settlement of South Africa and owns one of the newest design addresses of the country. The Bloomestate guesthouse is a new building. Clean, chic and cool, it is situated in the middle of rambling gardens and at the foot of the Langeberg Mountains. Depending on your mood and favorite color, you can take your pick of one of the seven rooms, which are designed according to the four seasons with clear lines and radiant colors. The Spring room beams in a fresh green, the Summer room creates atmosphere in sunset orange, a nostalgic purple reminds of the Fall, and in the Winter room a Nordic blue breeze finds its way onto the walls. Three other rooms in chocolate brown, gray-blue and romantic red are a tribute to earth, wind and fire. But whatever you decide: a luxury bathroom, television, minibar, i-pod music station and WLAN are standard in every room; as are the large doors which lead the way to the garden with pool and jacuzzi. Breakfast fans will find themselves on cloud nine at Bloomestate. And for romantic candlelight dinners the owners will be more than happy to recommend one of the nearby restaurants.

Swellendam, auf halbem Weg zwischen Kapstadt und der Garden Route zu finden, ist die drittälteste Siedlung Südafrikas und besitzt eine der jüngsten Designadressen des Landes. Das Gästehaus Bloomestate ist ein Neubau. Clean, schick und cool inmitten weitläufiger Gärten und am Fuß der Langeberg Mountains gelegen. Ganz nach Lust, Laune und Lieblingsfarbe kann man sich hier eines von sieben Zimmern aussuchen, die nach dem Motto der vier Jahreszeiten mit klaren Linien und leuchtenden Farben gestaltet sind. Das Frühlingszimmer strahlt in frischem Grün, sommerliche Stimmung schafft der Raum in Sonnenuntergangs-Orange, an den Herbst erinnert ein nostalgisches Purpur und der Winter schickt eine nordisch blaue Brise an die Wand. Drei weitere Zimmer in Schokoladenbraun, Graublau und Romantikrot sind eine Hommage an Erde, Wind und Feuer. Ganz egal, wie die Wahl ausfällt: ein Luxusbad, Fernseher, Minibar, i-pod Musikstation und WLAN sind in jedem Zimmer Standard; ebenso wie die großen Türen, die zum Garten mit Pool und Jacuzzi führen. Frühstücksfans leben auf Bloomestate wie im siebten Himmel. Und für das romantische Candlelight-Dinner empfehlen die Besitzer gerne eines der nahen Restaurants.

02

03

02 | Four seasons rooms—here is the Spring room in fresh green.

Vier-Jahreszeiten-Zimmer – hier das Frühlingszimmer in frischem Grün.

03 | A wonderful breakfast is served in the modern kitchen.

In der modernen Küche wird ein Frühstück vom Feinsten serviert.

04 | All rooms look directly out over the garden with its large pool and jacuzzi.

Alle Zimmer blicken direkt auf den Garten mit großem Pool und Jacuzzi.

01 | Natural stone and wood are the main materials at the lodge.

Naturstein und Holz sind die am meisten verwendeten Materialien der Lodge.

grootbos | hermanus-gansbaai . south africa

DESIGN: Vaughan Russell, Eloise Collocott-Russell, Dorothé Lutzeyer

Not far from the Cape of Good Hope is the Grootbos Private Nature Reserve, a haven of peace and relaxation for nature lovers. True to the Grootbos Foundation's commitment to nature conservation, there are no hordes of holidaymakers in this small paradise, just low-impact tourism. The same concept is also reflected in the design and architecture of the original, country-house-style Garden Lodge and the contemporary-style Forest Lodge, which was added only two years ago. There are 23 separate suites accessed via winding pathways through the Fynbos Park. Their interior decor is strikingly plain, playfully contrasting nature and civilization. The terraces look out onto the lush garden and the Fynbos Park, which extends to the dunes and cliffs at Walker Bay. It all seems virtually untouched, with penguins and seals playing about uninhibited in the water. 100 feet offshore it is even possible to see right whales swimming into this protected bay. While the adults are relaxing, swiming or taking a walk along the beaches, children enjoy a short adventure boat ride to the seal and whale colonies.

Unweit des Kap der guten Hoffnung finden Naturliebhaber im Grootbos Private Nature Reserve Ruhe und Entspannung. Eingebettet in das Naturschutz-Konzept der Grootbos Foundation gibt es in diesem kleinen Paradies keine Urlauber-Scharen, sondern nur sanften Tourismus. Dazu passt auch die Gestaltung und Philosophie, der ursprünglich im Landhausstil erbauten Garden Lodge und der erst vor zwei Jahren in zeitgenössischer Architektur hinzugefügten Forest Lodge. Zur Lodge gehören 23 separate Suiten, die über verschlungene Wege im Fynbos Park zu erreichen sind. Im spielerischen Kontrast zwischen Zivilisation und Natur wurden die Räume in einem betont sachlichen Stil eingerichtet. Die Terrassen bieten einen Blick auf den üppig bewachsenen Garten und in die Landschaft des Fynbos Parks. Dessen Vegetation reicht bis zu den Dünen und Klippen der Walker Bay. Alles wirkt beinahe unberührt, denn im Wasser tummeln sich ohne Scheu Pinguine und Robben. 30 Meter vom Ufer entfernt sieht man sogar Glattwale, die in diese geschützte Bucht kommen. Während sich die Erwachsenen an den langen Stränden beim Schwimmen oder bei Spaziergängen erholen, können die Kinder an kleinen Abenteuer-Bootsfahrten zu den Revieren der Robben und Wale teilnehmen.

02 | 03

02 | 03 The bar and lounge are in the main Grootbos Lodge building.

Im Haupthaus der Grootbos Lodge befinden sich Bar und Lounge.

04 | Guaranteed sunshine.
Ein Platz mit Sonnengarantie.

01 | The lounge with its reading room (left) and the gourmet restaurant (right) are surrounded by wooden terraces and water basins.

Umgeben von Holzterrassen und Wasserbecken befinden sich die Lounge mit Leseraum (links) sowie das Gourmetrestaurant (rechts).

tsala treetop lodge | plettenberg bay . south africa

DESIGN: Bruce Stafford and Hunter Family

If you want to stay on solid ground then you should find a different alternative to the Tsala Treetop Lodge. You want to aim high if you spend your vacation here: the lodge is hidden on stilts between the treetops of old giant jungle trees on the Garden Route. During your honeymoon you'll not only be undisturbed, but also a little bit closer to heaven. Created not far from the Tsitsikamma Mountains, these lodgings made of wood, natural stone and glass, the rustic structure that could easily misrepresent the great comfort of the lodge. In the ten tree house suites of the resort, as well as sleeping, living and bathrooms, is also a fireplace, in front of which you can snuggle up with one another on cold evenings or in winter. Every guest here is a baron on the trees: just one step from the suites and you'll be on one of the wooden walkways, which lead up through the forest to the main house with its restaurant, terraces and lobby and the other suites. The suites do not differ in their decor, but the design of the rooms is unique in every suite—local artists have decorated them with antique textiles and wood carvings. However, no extra decorations are actually needed against such a backdrop. A view out of the window or from the private open sky pool into the forest offers more in the blink of an eye, than ten stunning paintings at once.

Auf dem Teppich bleiben kann man an anderen Orten als in der Tsala Treetop Lodge. Denn wer hier seinen Urlaub verbringt, will hoch hinaus: die Lodge versteckt sich auf Stelzen zwischen den Wipfeln alter Urwaldriesen an der Garden Route. Während der Flitterwochen ist man so nicht nur ungestört, sondern kommt auch dem Himmel noch ein bisschen näher. Nicht weit vom Tsitsikamma-Berg entstand diese Unterkunft aus Holz, Naturstein und Glas, deren rustikale Bauart leicht über den großen Komfort der Lodge hinwegtäuschen könnte. In den zehn Baumhaus-Suiten der Anlage befindet sich jeweils neben Schlaf-, Wohn- und Badezimmer auch ein Kamin, vor dem man sich an kalten Abenden oder im Winter aneinanderschmiegen kann. Jeder Gast ist hier ein Baron auf den Bäumen: mit nur einem Schritt aus der Suite gelangt man auf einen der Holzstege, die hoch durch den Wald zum Haupthaus mit Restaurant, Terrassen sowie Lobby und den anderen Suiten führen. In ihrer Ausstattung unterscheiden sich die Suiten nicht, aber die Gestaltung der Räume ist in jeder Suite einzigartig – lokale Künstler haben sie mit antiken Textilien und Schnitzereien dekoriert. Eigentlich braucht man vor dieser Kulisse jedoch keine weiteren Verzierungen. Ein Blick aus dem Fenster oder vom Privatpool aus in die Wälder oder den offenen Himmel bietet mit einem einzigen Wimpernschlag mehr, als zehn umwerfende Gemälde auf einmal.

02 | Every treehouse suite has its own terrace with view over a ravine in the surrounding forests. Sometimes monkeys even pay a visit.

Jede Baumhaus-Suite hat ihre eigene Terrasse mit Ausblick über eine Schlucht auf die umliegenden Wälder. Manchmal kommen auch Affen zu Besuch.

03 | 04 Wood and quarrystone create a rustic, cozy atmosphere in the rooms.

Holz und Bruchstein sorgen für eine rustikal-gemütliche Atmosphäre in den Zimmern.

05 | You can relax in this bathtub, as well as in the private paddling pools.

Nicht nur im privaten Planschbecken, sondern auch in dieser Badewanne kann man entspannen.

taj lake palace | udaipur . india

DESIGN: James Park Associates

On your honeymoon and feeling like a maharaja? That might inspire some very high expectations. Nevertheless, those who select this palace as their domicile truly reside in the historic background of a 250 year-old summer residence of a Maharaja. Like its famous archetype, the Taj Mahal, the building is made of white marble—a light, long-stretching palace with small towers, cupolas, and rooftop terraces. It lies directly in Lake Pichola. Seen from the city of Udaipur, it looks as if a ship has dropped anchor here. Marble columns form the halls, the passages, ceilings and arched windows are entwined with rich decoration. Silks and frescos line the walls; elegant carvings make up the furnishings. The 100 accommodations are all luxury rooms and royal suites. That may seem surreal to some; others romanticize about it. Yet the hotel still manages to give this royal setting a contemporary elegance. Beside the waters, a lily pond fairytale garden surrounds the hotel. The emphasis here is that staying at the hotel is like staying on an island. A gondola transports the guests to the hotel—this is also a part of the romantic scenery surrounding the palace.

Flitterwochen und sich fühlen wie ein Maharadscha? Das mag nun doch zu hohe Erwartungen wecken. Dennoch, wer diesen Palast als Domizil auswählt, der logiert in der Tat in der historischen Kulisse einer 250 Jahre alten Sommerresidenz eines Maharadscha. Wie das berühmte Vorbild, das Taj Mahal, besteht das Gebäude aus weißem Marmor – ein heller, sich lang streckender Palast mit Türmchen, Kuppeln und Dachterrassen. Er liegt direkt im Picholasee. Von der Stadt Udaipur aus betrachtet scheint es, als hätte hier ein Schiff angelegt. Marmorsäulen prägen die Hallen. An den Durchgängen, Decken und Fensterbögen ranken sich reiche Verzierungen entlang. Seidenstoffe und bemalte Wände kleiden die Räume aus, Schnitzwerk bestimmt das alte Mobiliar. Die 100 Unterkünfte sind allesamt Luxuszimmer und Fürstensuiten. Das mag manch einem unwirklich erscheinen, andere geraten darüber ins Schwärmen. Doch dem Haus gelingt es, dem fürstlichen Rahmen durchaus zeitgemäße Eleganz zu verleihen. Abseits des Wassers umschließt ein Seerosenteich und Märchengarten das Hotel. So erlebt man beim Aufenthalt eine Art Inseldasein. Eine Gondel transportiert die Gäste zum Hotel – auch dies ist Teil der romantischen Inszenierung rund um diesen Palast.

01 | A palace made completely of marble, even the hand rails of the rooftop terrace.

Ein Palast ganz aus Marmor, bis hin zu den Brüstungen der Dachterrasse.

02 | Historical furnishings in the royal suites.

Historisches Mobiliar in den Fürstensuiten.

03 | The traditional adornments of the passageways are made of stained glass.

Die traditionellen Zierarbeiten der Durchgänge sind aus bemaltem Glas.

lighthouse hotel & spa | galle . sri lanka
DESIGN: Geoffrey Bawa

Surrounded by groves of palm trees on one side and the shimmering, clear, turquoise water of the Indian Ocean on the other side: What more could you dream of for that romantic getaway after just having tied the knot? The hotel complex built on a ledge near the city of Galle is found on a small, sandy bay along miles of sand beaches. The five star hotel is captivating thanks to its extraordinary architecture, simple elegance, and its picturesque location. When decorating the rooms special attention was paid to the gentle colors that dominate in the interior. All the rooms have a balcony or a terrace with a view to the sea, of course, exactly the right place to enjoy a cocktail and listen to sounds of sea or observe the surge meeting the shore. Active vacationers can enjoy everything from tennis and squash to billiards. If you would rather go on an adventure in the Indian Ocean, you can explore the underwater world by snorkeling and deep-sea diving. Or just relax your senses with an aromatherapy in the spa.

Umgeben von Palmenhainen auf der einen und dem glasklaren, türkisblau schimmernden Wasser des Indischen Ozeans auf der anderen Seite: Kann man sich mehr erträumen für das romantische Beisammensein, nachdem man den Bund fürs Leben geschlossen hat? Die auf einem Felsvorsprung erbaute Hotelanlage nahe der Stadt Galle liegt an einer kleinen Sandbucht entlang eines kilometerlangen Sandstrands. Das Fünf-Sterne-Haus besticht durch außergewöhnliche Architektur, schlichte Eleganz und seine malerische Lage. Bei der Ausstattung der Zimmer wurde besonders darauf geachtet, dass sanfte Farbtöne das Interieur dominieren. Sämtliche Zimmer verfügen über einen Balkon oder eine Terrasse – natürlich mit Meerblick, genau der richtige Ort, um bei einem Cocktail das Meeresrauschen zu genießen oder die Brandung zu beobachten. Sportlich Aktive können sich mit Tennis und Squash oder Billard vergnügen. Wer lieber im Indischen Ozean auf Entdeckungsreise gehen möchte, kann beim Schnorcheln oder Tauchen die Unterwasserwelt erkunden. Oder einfach nur die Seele baumeln lassen bei einer Aromatherapie im Spa.

01 | Stylish: The dark wood gives a sense of calm.

Stilvoll: Das dunkle Holz vermittelt ein Gefühl der Ruhe.

02 | You can even watch the ocean waves while swimming in the pool.

Beim Schwimmen im Pool kann man die Wellen des Ozeans beobachten.

03 | The hand railing, a work of art, that illustrates the history of Sri Lanka.

Das Treppengeländer – ein Kunstwerk, das die Geschichte Sri Lankas zeigt.

04 | The luxurious decor of the bathrooms meet even the highest demands.

Die luxuriöse Ausstattung der Badezimmer genügt höchsten Ansprüchen.

03 04

01 | The restaurant is located directly opposite to the pool in the garden.

Das Restaurant befindet sich vis-à-vis vom Gartenpool.

taru villas taprobana | bentota . sri lanka

DESIGN : Nayantara Fonseka, Taru; Rico

A special setting does not always have to be an oasis or a palace in order to make a destination more appealing. An intimate atmosphere is no less attractive. And maybe even more attractive if you are searching for a quaint and cozy nest for your honeymoon. The charm of the Taru Villas cannot be denied. They were designed by the most famous fashion designer and interior decorator in Sri Lanka. Some claim it to be a hip hotel; yet that truly does not describe the style of the hotel, more the guests that it attracts. The ensemble of the tract of houses is like country houses that one encounters in the Mediterranean area. Small but elegant luxury paraphrases the standards of their design—a search for evidence in the cultural fingerprints that were left behind by the colonial rulers. This is especially apparent in the nine individually furnished rooms: lattices and crates for doors, floors made of terracotta or cement, antiques interfused with modern interiors. The rooms with their balconies and terraces and the restaurant on the first floor are nestled around a garden with a pool, an informal situation to which the afternoon tea ceremony is obligatory. And: it is only a few steps to the beach which is often completely deserted.

Nicht immer muss es der besondere Rahmen einer Oase oder eines Palastes sein, damit von einer Destination Anziehungskraft ausgeht. Eine intime Atmosphäre ist nicht minder verlockend. Und vielleicht wirkt sie sogar umso attraktiver, wenn man sich auf der Suche nach einem beschaulichen Nest für seine Hochzeitsreise befindet. Diesen Charme kann man den Taru Villen nicht absprechen. Sie wurden von einem der bekanntesten Modedesigner und Innenausstatter Sri Lankas gestaltet. Ein hippes Hotel, wie manche behaupten, was aber weniger den Stil beschreibt, als wohl mehr auf die Gäste abzielt. Das Ensemble der Haustrakte gleicht Landhäusern, wie man sie aus dem Mittelmeerraum kennt. Kleiner, feiner Luxus umschreibt den Anspruch ihres Designs – eine Spurensuche in den kulturellen Abdrücken, die von den europäischen Kolonialherren hinterlassen wurden. Das zeigt sich vor allem in den neun individuell eingerichteten Zimmern: Gitter- und Holzverschläge als Türen, Böden aus Terrakotta oder Zement, Antiquitäten gemischt mit modernem Interieur. Diese Zimmer betten sich mit ihren Balkonen und Terrassen und dem Restaurant im Parterre um einen Garten mit Pool. Eine familiäre Situation, zu der die Zeremonie des Nachmittagstees obligatorisch gehört. Und: Nur wenige Schritte sind es bis zu einem oft menschenleeren Strand.

02   03

02 | A recurring theme in the design: old windows with crates as decorations.

Wiederkehrend im Design: alte Fenster mit Holzverschlägen als Dekor.

03 | A frameless bed focuses on a modern accent.

Das rahmenlose Bett setzt einen modernen Akzent.

04 | There has to be idyll: a sunken pond on the terrace.

Es geht nicht ohne Idylle: der eingelassene Teich auf der Terrasse.

04

kurumba maldives | male atoll . maldives
DESIGN: Mohamed Shafeeg, Mohamed Umar Maniku

This spot of nature was previously unpopulated. At the time it was called Vihamanaafushi, an island without poisonous plants. Then came the discovery of the special allure of the atoll, which is located near to the capital of Male with its airport. That was the beginning of the Kurumba resort more than 30 years ago. Meanwhile the resort takes up the entire 13 acres of the island, which doesn't mean anything: the bungalows and villas quietly assimilate into the dense vegetation. And so the coconut palms, luscious flowers and light sand remain an integral part of the charm of this destination. The pointed tiled roofs glimmer in the greenery, the buildings glow with their clear, white façades. Their interior design is especially modern and accentuated elegant, although it also reflects the traditions of the country. The dark floorboards act as a contrast to the light, warm tones of the walls. Standing dominant in the rooms are the four-poster beds. Wide windows and openings bring the nature into the ambience of the dwellings. Ten villas have a garden, eight their own pool. So much so that the island has become a resort and the resort an island, which now also bears the official name of Kurumba. Translated it means coconut village – a place, where you can watch the sun both rise and set in the same sea.

Früher war dieser Naturflecken noch unbesiedelt. Da hieß er Vihamanaa-fushi, Insel ohne Giftpflanzen. Dann entdeckte man den besonderen Reiz des Atolls, das nahe an der Hauptstadt Male mit seinem Flughafen liegt. Das war der Beginn des Kurumba Resorts – vor über 30 Jahren. Mittlerweile nimmt die Anlage die gesamten fünf Hektar des Eilandes ein, was aber nichts heißen will: Die Bungalows und Villen fügen sich eher zurückhaltend in die dichte Vegetation ein. So bilden die Kokospalmen, üppigen Blumen und der helle Sand einen wesentlichen Teil des Charmes, der von dieser Destination ausgeht. Die spitzen Ziegeldächer schimmern aus dem Grün heraus, die Gebäude strahlen mit ihrer klaren weißen Fassade. Ihre Einrichtung wirkt vor allem modern und betont elegant, wenngleich sie auch die Traditionen des Landes widerspiegelt. Die Böden sind aus dunklen Dielen und werden von den hellen, warmen Tönen der Wände kontrastiert. Dominant stehen Himmelbetten im Raum. Weite Fenster und Öffnungen holen die Natur ins Ambiente der Behausungen hinein. Zehn Villen besitzen dazu einen Garten, acht einen eigenen Pool. Die Insel ist zum Resort geworden und das Resort zur Insel, die nun auch offiziell den Namen Kurumba trägt. Übersetzt heißt es Kokosnussdorf – ein Platz, an dem man die Sonne im gleichen Meer aufsteigen und untergehen sieht.

01 | The Beach Villa: pictures tell of life and work on the Maldives.

Die Beach Villa: Bilder erzählen vom Leben und Arbeiten auf den Malediven.

02 | The slinky shapes of the pool draw in the surrounding nature.

Die geschmeidigen Formen des Pools zeichnen sich in der umgebenden Natur ab.

03 | The corner seating, sunk into the floor, alludes to the seating traditions of the region.

Die im Boden eingelassene Sitzecke spielt auf die Sitztradition der Region an.

04 | The modern tiled roofs interpret the pagoda shape in a new way.

Die modernen Ziegeldächer interpretieren die Pagodenform neu.

05 | Dominantly placed and romantic: an old-fashioned four-poster bed.

Dominant platziert und romantisch: ein Himmelbett im alten Stil.

03 04

05

sila evason hideaway & spa at samui | koh samui . thailand

DESIGN: Team around Eva Shivdasani, Amata Luphaiboon

If there is a couple, who can claim to have discovered the honeymoon hotel, then it is Sonu and Eva Shivdasani. When the British business man with Indian roots and the Swedish model met in the 80's, hideaways for lovers had not come very far. Without further ado Sonu eased a Maldive island, where he built a luxury resort for his Eva. The foundation stone to a small chain had been laid. Nowadays the pair doesn't just run little paradises in the island idyll of the Maldives, but also in Vietnam and Thailand. Sila Evason Hideaway lies on the north tip of Koh Samui, right on the sea and amidst tropical nature. 66 villas were built here on the hillside. Picture book panorama and privacy are guaranteed here. Inside an ornately gathered mosquito net billows over the bed. On awakening you will look straight out over the ocean. Interfering accessories, which could steal the show from such artistic impressions, are done without here. The few furnishings made of dark wood and fabrics in light colors suffice. The feeling of space and expanse is also underlined by the open-plan bathrooms and the infinity pools. What more could one need for a wonderful week à deux? Just a spa and excellent restaurants; and Sonu and Eva have thought of both—proving that they are honeymoon experts.

Wenn es ein Paar gibt, das von sich behaupten darf, das Honeymoon Hotel erfunden zu haben, dann Sonu und Eva Shivdasani. Denn als sich der britische Geschäftsmann mit indischen Wurzeln und das schwedische Model in den 80er Jahren kennenlernten, war es mit den Hideaways für Verliebte noch nicht weit her. Sonu pachtete kurzerhand eine Malediven-Insel und baute dort seiner Eva ein Luxusresort. Der Grundstein zu einer kleinen Kette war gelegt. Heute betreiben die beiden nicht nur in der Inselidylle der Malediven kleine Paradiese, sondern auch in Vietnam und Thailand. Sila Evason Hideaway liegt an der Nordspitze von Koh Samui, direkt am Meer und inmitten tropischer Natur. 66 Villen wurden hier an den Hang gebaut. Bilderbuch-Panorama und Privatsphäre sind garantiert. Innen bauscht sich über dem Bett ein kunstvoll gerafftes Moskitonetz. Beim Aufwachen blickt man direkt auf den Ozean. Auf störende Accessoires, die solchen Impressionen die Show stehlen könnten, wird verzichtet. Die wenigen Möbel aus dunklem Holz und mit Stoffen in hellen Farben genügen sich selbst. Das Gefühl von Raum und Weite unterstreichen auch die Open-style-Bäder und die Infinity-Pools. Was braucht man mehr für wunderbare Wochen zu zweit? Nur ein Spa und exzellente Restaurants; und an beides haben Sonu und Eva gedacht – Honeymoon-Experten eben.

01 | Eco-chic thanks to the high windows, dark wood and light fabrics.
Eco-Chic dank hoher Fenster, dunklem Holz und heller Stoffe.

02 | The turquoise blue of the infinity pools seems to flow right into the sky and the sea.

Das Türkisblau des Infinitypools scheint direkt in den Himmel und ins Meer zu fließen.

03 | The bathrooms made of wood and stone also open up a panorama into paradise.

Auch die Bäder aus Holz und Stein eröffnen ein Panorama ins Paradies.

01 | Western design fuses with Malaysian handicrafts.

Westliches Design verbindet sich mit malaiischem Kunsthandwerk.

four seasons resort langkawi | langkawi . malaysia
DESIGN: Bill Bensley from Bensley Design Studios, Lek Bunnag from Bunnag Architects

Tropical oases have always been enticing. Langkawi is one of those places. An island group of 99 pieces of land projecting out of the water, covered by a rainforest and bathed by the Andamanen Sea. Amidst this natural beauty the hideaway has chosen one of the most beautiful beaches: Tanjung Rhu. On entering the central pavilion with its long veranda front, you'll be reminded of a Buddhist temple. The roof made of shingles, wood carvings stretches along and the lamps resemble the tips of pagodas. The light of three rows of lanterns spectacularly reflects on the wall in the water of a fountain. Therein lies the philosophy of the house: to provide space for peculiarities of the regional architecture and yet also to offer Western luxury and comfort. Malaysian artists were involved in the design of the 68 pavilion rooms and 22 villas. The baths can be found under a glass dome and are made from heavily grained marble from Spain. Art and fragrant candles add to the decoration. This form of idyllic alcoves characterizes the house and is a tranquil invitation to all romantic souls—especially in the six wellness pavilions surrounded by high granite rocks of the spa, which are grouped around a lotus pond.

Von je her locken tropische Oasen. Langkawi ist so ein Ort. Eine Inselgruppe aus 99 versprengt aus dem Wasser ragenden Landstücken, vom Regenwald überzogen und umspült vom Andamanischen Meer. Im Umfeld dieser Naturschönheiten suchte sich dieser Hideaway einen der schönsten Strände aus: Tanjung Rhu. Wer den zentralen Pavillon mit seiner langen Verandafront betritt, der mag sich an einen buddhistischen Tempel erinnert fühlen. Lang zieht sich das Dach aus Schindeln, Schnitzwerk ist zu sehen und die Lampen ähneln den Spitzen von Pagoden. Eindrucksvoll spiegelt sich im Wasser eines Brunnens das Licht von drei Laternenreihen an der Wand. Die Philosophie des Hauses: Eigenheiten der regionalen Architektur Raum geben und doch Luxus und Komfort westlicher Prägung offerieren. Malaiische Künstler wirkten bei der Gestaltung der 68 Pavillonzimmer und 22 Villen mit. Die Bäder umspannen Glaskuppeln und bestehen aus stark gemasertem Marmor aus Spanien. Kleinkunst und Duftkerzen schmücken sie. Diese Form idyllischer Nischen prägt das Haus und ist eine stille Einladung an alle romantischen Seelen – ganz besonders in den sechs von hohen Granitfelsen umrahmten Wellness-Pavillons im Spa, die sich um einen Lotusteich gruppieren.

03 04

02 | A charming light shrine in the inner courtyard of the resort.

Ein anmutiger Lichtschrein im Innenhof des Resorts.

03 | Lamps, furniture and decoration come from local artists.

Lampen, Möbel und Dekor stammen von einheimischen Künstlern.

04 | Modern style and comfort can be found in the king size beds and curtains.

Moderner Stil und Komfort zeigen sich an den Kingsize-Betten und Vorhängen.

01 | The cabana is open on three sides. You can sit here in the
evenings too thanks to the mild temperatures.

Die Cabana ist nach drei Seiten offen. Dank der milden
Temperaturen kann man hier auch abends entspannt sitzen.

alila ubud | bali . indonesia
DESIGN: Kerry Hill

If there were a ranking of the 50 best hotel pools in the world then Alila Ubud would be right at the top. Coming from the pool bar, you enter the cool depths and the water seems to flow through an endless terraced jungle that reaches all the way to the sky. The trick to it is quite easy: it is built on the edge of a river valley. Right at the edge of the edgeless head part, the sacred Ayung River makes a sharp curve and continues to flow in the same alignment as the anthracite-colored pool. You could get the impression from this view of the water´s surface that it is a viaduct over the river valley, enclosed on the left and right by forest-covered hills. The hotel is located approximately 12 miles from the artist village, Ubud, an exposed area between the tropical forest and rice fields. The complex planned by Kerry Hill Architects and run by the small but exclusive hotel group Alila Hotels has 56 rooms in the solidly constructed "town houses" and eight villas that are built on stilts like tree houses above the river valley. In style of a small village there are 14 two-story blocks, each with four units. There the smooth plaster walls and concrete meet thatched roofs, terracotta tiles meet gravel and crushed rock, wood meets glass. Traditional architecture is combined with contemporary style. And where still life hangs on the walls in other hotels, the Alila Ubud simply leaves the windows open.

Gäbe es ein Ranking der 50 besten Hotelpools der Welt, wäre das Alila Ubud ganz vorne mit dabei. Steigt man von der Poolbar kommend ins Wasser und legt zum Schwimmen an, scheint er endlos durch den Dschungel in den Himmel zu reichen. Dabei ist der Trick ganz einfach: Er ist bis an den Rand einer Schlucht gebaut. Genau unterhalb des randlosen Kopfendes schlägt der heilige Ayung Fluss eine scharfe Biegung und verläuft weiter in der gleichen Flucht wie der anthrazitfarbene Pool. In Sichthöhe der Wasseroberfläche entsteht der Eindruck, als wäre er ein Viadukt über dem Flusstal, links und rechts besäumt von bewaldeten Hügeln. Das Hotel liegt rund acht Kilometer entfernt vom Künstlerort Ubud an exponierter Stelle, zwischen Tropenwald und Reisfeldern. Die von Kerry Hill geplante und von der kleinen aber feinen indonesischen Hotelgruppe Alila Hotels betriebene Anlage hat 56 Zimmer in massiv gebauten „Reihenhäuschen" und acht Villen, die auf Stelzen wie Baumhäuser über der Schlucht stehen. Im Stil einer kleinen Siedlung, gibt es entlang der Schlucht 14 zweigeschossige Blocks mit jeweils vier Wohneinheiten. Dort treffen glatte Putzwände und Beton auf Strohdächer, Terrakottaplatten auf Kiesel- und Bruchsteine und Holz auf Glas. Traditionelle Bauweisen werden so mit zeitgnössischem Stil verknüpft. Und wo in anderen Hotels impressionistische Stillleben an den Wänden hängen, hat man im Alila Ubud einfach die Fenster offen gelassen.

02 03

02 | The sleeping quarters in one of the villas. The wood terrace
     beyond the sliding glass door lies directly above the Ayung Gorge.

     Schlafraum in einer der Villen. Die Holzterrasse hinter der Glas-
     Falttüre liegt direkt über der Ayung-Schlucht.

03 | Open living is a basic principle of Balinese architecture. In the
     villas even the bath rooms are outdoors.

     Offenes Wohnen ist ein Grundprinzip der balinesischen
     Architektur. In den Villen zählt dazu auch das Bad im Freien.

04 | From the perspective of the water's surface, the swimming
     pool seems to blend into the treetops then into infinity. An
     architectural masterpiece.

     Aus der Perspektive der Wasseroberfläche verliert sich der
     Pool zwischen den Baumwipfeln in der Unendlichkeit. Eine
     architektonische Meisterleistung.

01 | The resort is located opposite the Otemanu Mountain.

Das Resort liegt vis-à-vis vom Berg Otemanu.

st. regis resort bora bora | bora bora . french polynesia

DESIGN: Pierre Lacombe, Miriam Hall

When far and wide travelers talk about the South Pacific and the name Bora Bora crops up in conversation, their eyes normally light up. The allure of the rugged archipelago, the seclusion of the lagoons, the shimmering of the water all stir longing. And if there is also the promise of luxurious accommodation, then even Hollywood stars like Nicole Kidman and Keith Urban would come to join the rest of the honeymoon couples. We're talking about the St. Regis Resort Bora Bora, which opened in summer 2006. Villas with private helipad signify the demands of the destination: island luxury of an extra class. The suites are mainly bungalows above the water—stilt houses typical of the country—or isolated on the beach. The smallest of them measures 1,600 square-feet, the largest 13,000 square-feet. There are one, two or three bedrooms—in the style of urban comfort, emphasized with wood, polished floorboards, dark furniture and handmade fabrics. Private open air showers on the terrace are standard, whirlpools or a private pool sunk into the lagoon are part of the high quality facilities. Also the restaurant floats above the water. Spa and fitness center are housed in a peaceful retreat on a neighboring island. And every bungalow has a personal butler to attend to those who still have any wishes.

Wenn Viel- und Weitgereiste über die Südsee sprechen und der Name Bora Bora fällt, blitzt zumeist ein Leuchten in ihren Augen auf. Der Reiz des zerklüfteten Archipels, die Abgeschiedenheit der Lagunen, das Schimmern des Wassers weckt Sehnsüchte. Wenn dann noch das Versprechen einer luxuriösen Unterbringung gegeben wird, dann stellen sich selbst Hollywoodstars wie Nicole Kidman und Keith Urban als Flitterwochen-Paar ein. Die Rede ist vom St. Regis Resort Bora Bora, im Sommer 2006 eröffnet. Villen mit privatem Hubschrauber-Landeplatz deuten die Ansprüche der Destination an: Inselluxus der Extraklasse. Die Suiten sind zum großen Teil als Bungalows über dem Wasser gebaut – landestypische Pfahlbauten – oder liegen vereinzelt am Strand. Die kleinste von ihnen misst 145 Quadratmeter, die größte 1210 Quadratmeter. Es gibt ein, zwei oder drei Schlafzimmer – im Stil urbanen Komforts, holzbetont, mit geschliffenen Dielen, dunklen Möbeln und handgearbeiteten Stoffen. Sichtgeschützte Freiduschen auf der Terrasse gehören zum Standard, Whirlpools oder ein in die Lagune eingelassener Privatpool zur gehobenen Ausstattung. Auch das Restaurant schwebt über dem Wasser. Spa und Fitness-Center sind als stilles Refugium auf einer benachbarten Insel untergebracht. Und wenn dann noch Wünsche offen bleiben, steht für jeden Bungalow ein persönlicher Butler bereit.

02 | The private pools are sunk into the lagoon.

Die privaten Pools sind in die Lagune eingelassen.

03 | Polished tropical woods and fabrics denote the furnishings.

Polierte tropische Hölzer und Stoffe kennzeichnen die Ausstattung.

04 | The open plan living room leads straight to your own beach garden.

Vom offenen Wohnzimmer geht der Weg direkt in den eigenen Strandgarten.

02

03

04

vatulele island resort | vatulele island . fiji

DESIGN: Martin Livingston, Doug Nelson, Henry Crawford

On this lonely island the figures speak for themselves: the resort offers space for just 19 married couples, who are looked after by 110 employees. But the estate doesn't just set benchmarks in terms of service, but also in design. The large villas combine colors and fabrics of the South Pacific with shapes from Europe. This corresponds to the personalities of the owners, who come from Australia and Fiji and have European roots. And so the sunshine yellow villas fit perfectly into the untouched landscape. Inside tree logs, which have been weathered by the sun and the sea are used as sculptures. The furniture with its clear, minimal lines has more of a European tradition. The classic honeymoon villa is pink, 2,000 square-feet large and as well as a private pool and a large free standing bathtub, it has four showers—two inside and two outside. Protection from unwanted glances is offered by the original, tropical forest, which surrounds every villa. It is however still only a short walk to the main house. Of course everything is included in this hotel. The only thing the guests have to do without is their shoes. Walking barefoot is etiquette here. This is after all the best way to feel the fine, white sand under your feet.

Zahlen sprechen auf dieser einsamen Insel für sich: Das Resort bietet Platz für 19 Hochzeitspaare, um die sich 110 Angestellte kümmern. Doch nicht nur in puncto Service, sondern auch im Design setzt das Anwesen Maßstäbe. Die großzügig geschnittenen Villen verbinden Farben und Materialien der Südsee mit Formen aus Europa. Das entspricht der Persönlichkeit der Besitzer, die aus Australien und Fidschi kommen und europäische Wurzeln haben. So passen die sonnengelben Villen perfekt in die unberührte Landschaft. Innen werden von Sonne und Meer gegerbte Baumstämme als Skulpturen eingesetzt. Das Mobiliar steht mit seinen klaren, reduzierten Linien eher in europäischer Tradition. Die klassische Flitterwochen-Villa ist rosa, 180 Quadratmeter groß und bietet neben einem privaten Pool und einer großen frei stehenden Badewanne, vier Duschen – zwei im Inneren, zwei im Freien. Schutz vor ungewollten Einblicken bietet der ursprüngliche, tropische Wald, der jede Villa umgibt. Zum Haupthaus ist es trotzdem nur ein kurzer Fußweg. Im Hotel ist selbstverständlich alles inklusive. Nur auf ihre Schuhe müssen die Gäste verzichten. Barfuss laufen gehört zum guten Ton. Schließlich lässt sich so auch am besten der feine, weiße Sand unter den Füßen spüren.

01 | The most expensive villa of the resort boasts two private pools.

Zwei private Pools gehören zur teuersten Villa des Resorts.

02 | Living and bedroom are just separated from one another by three steps.

Wohn- und Schlafzimmer sind nur drei Stufen voneinander getrennt.

03 | Exactly twelve doors lead from every "Deluxe Beach Bure" to the private terrace.

Exakt zwölf Türen führen von jeder „Deluxe Beach Bure" auf die private Terrasse.

04 | Guests have a sea view from almost all rooms in the sublimely located "The Point" villa.

Von nahezu allen Zimmern in der erhaben gelegenen Villa „The Point" hat der Gast Meerblick.

01 | The house is located right in the middle of an almost
24 hectare large park.

Das Haus liegt inmitten eines knapp 24 Hektar großen Parks.

mayflower inn & spa | washington . connecticut
DESIGN: Randall Ridless

A crackling fire, a cozy armchair and a hot cup of tea—all of these three things are linked to the house. This is why it's the ideal place for honeymoons in the fall and winter. Whilst colorful leaves or snowflakes are falling outside, the guests can make themselves really cozy inside. The 30 rooms of the luxurious country house are divided into four buildings. Every room is individually decorated, but they all have one thing in common: opulence. Heavy, noble fabrics adorn the four-poster beds and frame the windows. Armchairs and sofas are thickly upholstered. Artworks from the 18th and 19th centuries decorate the walls. The spacious bathrooms are decked out in marble and mahogany. The bathtubs, according to the hotel management, are so deep, that all of your stresses will be drowned away in them. After a long bath guests can relax in the antique beds, enjoy the fireplace or watch the latest films on the plasma televisions. But the nearby surroundings are also of interest. Rambling, riding, tennis and golf are on the agenda. In close vicinity is the unspoilt, spectacular Steeprock Nature Reserve. If you have worn yourself out there you can have your tired muscles massaged in the 19,000 square-feet spa.

Ein knisterndes Feuer, ein gemütlicher Sessel und heißer Tee – diese drei Dinge sind untrennbar mit dem Haus verbunden. Damit ist es der ideale Ort für Flitterwochen im Herbst und Winter. Während draußen bunte Blätter oder Schneeflocken fallen, können es sich die Gäste drinnen so richtig gemütlich machen. Die 30 Räume des luxuriösen Landhauses sind auf vier Gebäude verteilt. Jedes Zimmer ist individuell eingerichtet, doch eins haben alle gemeinsam: die Opulenz. Schwere, edle Stoffe zieren die Himmelbetten und umrahmen die Fenster. Sessel und Sofas sind dick gepolstert. Kunstwerke aus dem 18. und 19. Jahrhundert schmücken die Wände. Die geräumigen Badezimmer sind mit Marmor und Mahagoni ausgekleidet. Die Badewannen sind nach Aussage der Hotelleitung so tief, dass der gesamte Stress in ihnen ertrinkt. Nach einem ausgiebigen Bad können die Gäste in den antiken Betten entspannen, das Kaminfeuer genießen oder auf dem Flachbildschirm die neuesten Filme ansehen. Doch auch die Umgebung ist reizvoll. Wandern, Reiten, Tennis und Golf stehen auf dem Programm. In unmittelbarer Nähe liegt das unberührte, spektakuläre Steeprock Naturreservat. Wer sich dort verausgabt hat, kann sich anschließend die müden Muskeln im 1800 Quadratmeter großen Spa massieren lassen.

02 | Even the spa has its own fireplace, where guests can warm up after swimming.

Sogar das Spa hat einen eigenen Kamin, an dem sich die Gäste nach dem Schwimmen aufwärmen können.

03 | As a welcome gift visitors will find orchids in their rooms.

Orchideen finden die Besucher als Willkommensgruß in allen Zimmern.

04 | The chefs prefer to use local, organic ingredients.

Die Köche verwenden bevorzugt lokale, biologische Zutaten.

03

04

wheatleigh | lenox . massachusetts
DESIGN: Calvin Tsao, Zack McKown

The house in the Florentine palazzo style stands at a prominent location: a lake stretches out beyond the foot of a bank. It enables a good view of the Berkshire countryside, one of the most popular tourist regions in the northern part of the state. Every year in the summer, the nearby town of Lenox accommodates the Boston Symphony Orchestra. Nevertheless, the hotel also represents a place with its own appeal. Above all what is meant: the imposing architecture of an Italian castle in the country. It was built in 1893 and served as a private villa for many years. Following a complete renovation, it now receives hotel guests. It opens up accommodations to them full of traditional luxury with sculpture gardens, fountains, and colonnades. The Tiffany windows show flower motifs. High arches span the windows and openings. The 19 rooms and suites have fireplaces made of limestone and decorated with stucco. Furniture and decorations discreetly emphasize the "grandezza". The baths are charming with old sinks made of marble and bathtubs on high, decorative pedestals. The rooms on the upper level lead directly out to a veranda or a rooftop garden. The grand hall in the center of the palace should also be mentioned. It often serves as a grand location for a wedding celebration.

Das Haus im Stile eines florentinischen Palazzos steht an prominenter Stelle: eine Anhöhe, zu deren Füßen sich ein See erstreckt. Sie eröffnet eine gute Sicht über die Landschaft des Berkshires, einer gern bereisten Region in dem nördlichen Bundesstaat. Jedes Jahr im Sommer beherbergt die nahe Stadt Lenox das Bostoner Symphonieorchester. Doch davon abgesehen stellt auch das Hotel einen Ort von eigenem Reiz dar, vor allem seine imposante Architektur eines italienischen Landschlosses. Errichtet wurde es im Jahre 1893 und diente lange als private Villa. Nach einer umfassenden Renovierung empfängt das Haus nun aber Hotelgäste. Denen eröffnet es eine Unterkunft voll von althergebrachtem Luxus mit Skulpturengarten, Wasserspielen und Kolonnaden. Die Tiffany-Fenster zeigen zarte Blumenmotive. Hohe Bögen umspannen Fenster und freie Öffnungen. Die 19 Zimmer und Suiten besitzen mit Stuck verzierte Feuerstellen. Möbel und Dekorationen unterstreichen dezent die Grandezza. Charmant sind die Bäder: mit alten Waschtischen aus Marmor und Wannen auf verschnörkelten Füßen. Die oberen Räume führen direkt auf eine Veranda oder einen Dachgarten. Hinweisen sollte man aber auch auf die große Halle im Zentrum des Palastes. Sie dient häufig als würdevoller Ort für eine Hochzeitsgesellschaft.

01 | Suite on the upper floor with direct access to the veranda.

Suite im oberen Stock mit direktem Zugang zur Veranda.

2 | Bathtub and sink give the bathrooms a historical ambiance.

Wanne und Waschtisch geben dem Ambiente der Bäder historisches Flair.

3 | The spiral staircase leads to the sleeping chambers.

Die Wendeltreppe führt hinauf zum Schlafgemach.

04 | 05

04 | A bright place: the restaurant with high windows and mirrors.

Ein lichter Ort: das Restaurant mit hohen Fenstern und Spiegeln.

05 | The fireplaces are framed by elaborate reliefs and sculptures made of limestone.

Die Kamine sind umrahmt von aufwändigen Reliefs und Skulpturarbeiten.

06 | Even the fountain is from the year 1893, as well as the Florentine Palazzo.

Auch der Brunnen ist aus dem Jahre 1893 – so wie der florentinische Palazzo.

amanyara | providenciales . turks and caicos

DESIGN: Team around Jean Michel Gathy

The name of Amanyara is translated as "peaceful place". So guests know what awaits them before they have even arrived. The design becomes one with the landscape and consciously plays with natural elements, like the refreshing sea breeze, the lapping of the waves and the rays of sunshine. So in the 40 pavilions of the resort the outside areas are just as important, as the rooms inside. The three terraces of every small villa are equipped with cozy white lounger furniture. You'll be searching to no avail for Caribbean clichés here. Clear lines, white, light wood and chrome define the image. In the living spaces guests will find a bar, a bathroom with a free-standing bathtub and a separate dressing room. The houses are scattered on the tropically forested area or stand on stilts in the ocean and are connected with wooden walkways. And in the communal areas the guests can also choose between open spaces right by the sea and climatized interiors. Attractive views can be admired from everywhere. The restaurant, bar, boutique and bookstore are grouped around the elaborate layout of the pool, where the old trees create shade. If you prefer the sea, you can vitalize yourself with fresh fruits at the Beach Club, before heading off to discover the endless beach.

Friedlicher Ort lautet die Übersetzung des Namens Amanyara. Da weiß der Gast bereits vor seiner Ankunft, was ihn erwartet. Das Design bildet eine Einheit mit der Landschaft und spielt ganz bewusst mit natürlichen Elementen wie der frischen Meeresbrise, dem Rauschen der Wellen und den Sonnenstrahlen. So sind bei den 40 Pavillons des Resorts die Außenbereiche mindestens ebenso wichtig, wie die Räume im Inneren. Die drei Terrassen jeder kleinen Villa sind mit gemütlichen weißen Lounge-möbeln ausgestattet. Karibische Klischees sucht man hier vergebens. Klare Linien, Weiß, helles Holz und Chrom bestimmen das Bild. In den Wohnräumen findet der Gast eine Bar, ein Bad mit frei stehender Bade-wanne und ein separates Ankleidezimmer. Die Häuser liegen verstreut auf dem tropisch bewaldeten Gelände oder stehen auf Stelzen im Meer und sind mit Holzstegen verbunden. Auch bei den gemeinschaftlich genutzten Bereichen können die Gäste zwischen offenen Aufenthaltsflächen direkt am Meer und klimatisierten Innenräumen wählen. Attraktive Ausblicke bieten sich von überall. So gruppieren sich Restaurant, Bar, Boutique und Bücherei um den aufwendig angelegten Pool, an dem alte Bäume Schatten spenden. Wer das Meer vorzieht, kann sich im Beach Club mit frischen Früchten stärken, bevor er zur Erkundung des endlosen Strandes aufbricht.

01 | The hotel's countless terraces offer the perfect views of the protected coral reef.

Den perfekten Blick auf das unter Naturschutz stehende Korallenriff bieten die unzähligen Terrassen des Hotels.

02 | If you'd always wanted to own a house on the beach, you can at least
make this dream come true on your honeymoon.

Wer schon immer ein eigenes Haus am Strand besitzen wollte, kann
diesen Traum zumindest auf seiner Hochzeitsreise wahr machen.

03 | Guests can plan their next spa treatment, dive and golf game over a relaxed fruit cocktail on their own terrace.

Das nächste Spa-Treatment, den Tauchausflug und das Golfmatch kann der Gast ganz entspannt bei einem Fruchtcocktail auf der eigenen Terrasse planen.

04 | The pavilions are not just reminiscent of a New York loft apartment, but they also offer the same comfort.

Die Pavillons erinnern nicht nur an eine New Yorker Loft-Wohnung, sondern bieten auch denselben Komfort.

01 | The extraordinary architecture lets the boundaries between the
interior and exterior melt away.

Die außergewöhnliche Architektur lässt die Grenzen zwischen
drinnen und draußen verschwimmen.

hix island house | vieques . puerto rico

DESIGN: John Hix

Giant, gray granite boulders that set themselves apart from the tropical landscape and yet harmonize with it at the same time were the inspiration for the architect, John Hix. His goal when designing the Hix Island House was to present guests from all over the world with something they had never seen before. Hix mainly used concrete for the construction of the four buildings in which 13 completely furnished apartments are found. These shimmer matt gray in the middle of the surrounding vegetation burts with color. The concrete dominates both the geometrical façades as well as the interiors. Inside the walls seem partially like sculptures. Stairs seem to lead no where. Other decorative elements are thus superfluous. Large unglazed panorama windows give the landscape a monumental appearance. Numerous old trees not only give shade but also a sense of calm on the over 12,000 acres of land. The rooms have neither telephones nor televisions; harmony with nature is a central theme. Solar collectors and a rain water treatment collectors are of course part of the fixtures at this ecologically-minded resort. Each of the individual houses with rolling steel doors and heavy wooden shutters also offers protection against the elements. The minimalist, rustic rooms offer the guest one thing above all—space for their own thoughts.

Riesige graue Granitblöcke, die sich von der tropischen Landschaft abheben und sie gleichzeitig formen, lieferten die Inspiration für Architekt John Hix. Sein Ziel bei der Gestaltung des Hix Island House war es, Gästen von überall auf der Welt etwas noch nie Gesehenes zu präsentieren. Für den Bau der vier Häuser, in denen 13 voll ausgestattete Apartments untergebracht sind, nutzte Hix vorwiegend Beton. Dieser schimmert mattgrau inmitten der vor intensiven Farben strotzenden Vegetation. Der Beton dominiert sowohl die geometrischen Fassaden, als auch die Innenräume. Dort wirken die Wände zum Teil skulpturartig. Treppen scheinen ins Nichts zu führen. Weitere dekorative Elemente sind somit fast überflüssig. Riesige unverglaste Panoramafenster lassen auch die Landschaft monumental erscheinen. Auf über fünf Hektar spenden unzählige alte Bäume nicht nur Schatten, sondern auch Ruhe. Die Zimmer haben weder Telefon noch Fernseher, der Einklang mit der Natur ist ein zentrales Element. Solarzellen und eine Wasseraufbereitungsanlage gehören selbstverständlich zur Ausstattung des ökobewussten Resorts. Mit rollenden Stahltüren und massiven Holzfensterläden bieten die einzelnen Häuser aber auch Schutz vor Naturgewalten. Dem Gast geben die minimalistisch rustikalen Zimmer vor allem eins – Raum für eigene Gedanken.

05

02 | For breakfast, there is homemade bread and locally grown coffee.

Zum Frühstück gibt es hausgemachtes Brot und Kaffee, der in der Umgebung angebaut wird.

03 | Not only can guests relax on the large sun terrace but also practicing yoga in the Yoga Pavilion that was created especially for this purpose.

Entspannen kann der Gast nicht nur auf der großen Sonnenterrasse, sondern auch beim Yoga im speziell dafür angelegten Yoga-Pavillon.

04 | The reduced design is accentuated by colorful fabrics, which where imported from Europe.

Das reduzierte Design wird durch bunte Stoffe akzentuiert, die aus Europa stammen.

05 | From the geometric pool, the Caribbean beach is only a few minutes away.

Vom geometrischen Pool zum karibischen Strand sind es nur wenige Minuten.

casa colonial | puerto plata . dominican republic

DESIGN: Sarah Garcia

In the background of the hotel, mighty mangroves rise up out of the swamp casting their shadows. In the foreground the hotel with its lobby and lounge appears in view: a new building that is presented in the typical Caribbean colonial style. A gleaming white façade at the entrance. The side wings are moved slightly forward. A veranda on the first floor encircles the inner courtyard over which tiled roofs hang—a cool, bright spot to relax with a good book. The hotel gives off an elegant, friendly atmosphere. Especially the public areas prove to be real treasures. You walk across a shining polished sandstone floor. The stonework framed in white is made of the same material. Enticingly modern, the wine cellar, with a shelf built directly into the wall. As is true with the gourmet restaurant Lucia, it stages young, sculptural art as well. A pool deck and four whirlpools on the rooftop allow for relaxing time with a panorama view of the dense vegetation and the sea. All of the lodgings are furnished as suites, different in size yet the same in style: oversized colonial beds, romantically lit with large candles. The same is true for the bathtubs in the spacious bathrooms. The motto of the house: there shall be no want for comfort.

Im Hintergrund des Hotels ragen mächtige Mangroven auf, die sich aus einem Sumpf erheben. Sie werfen Schatten herüber. Davor rückt das Haus mit Lobby und Lounge in den Blick: ein neuer Bau, der sich im typischen Kolonialstil der Karibik präsentiert. Eine strahlend weiße Fassade im Entree. Etwas vorgerückt sind Seitenflügel. Eine Veranda über die sich Ziegeldächer spannen umzieht im Innenhof den ersten Stock – kühle, helle Plätze, um sich mit einem Buch zurückzuziehen. Das Haus verströmt eine geschmackvolle, freundliche Atmosphäre. Vor allem die öffentlichen Räume erweisen sich als elegante Kleinode. Man wandelt über einen glänzend polierten Sandstein. Aus dem gleichen Material besteht auch das weiß gerahmte Mauerwerk. Verlockend modern: der Weinkeller, mit einem in die Wand eingelassenen Regal. Er inszeniert, genauso wie das Gourmetrestaurant Lucia, junge skulpturale Kunst. Pooldeck und vier Whirlpools auf dem Dach eröffnen lässige Stunden mit weitem Blick über die dichte Vegetation und das Meer. Die Unterkünfte sind alle als Suiten eingerichtet; unterschiedlich in der Größe, im Stil aber gleich: überdimensionale Kolonialbetten, romantisch beleuchtet mit großen Kerzen. Gleiches gilt für die Wannen in den großzügigen Bädern. An Komfort soll es nicht mangeln, ist das Credo des Hauses.

01 | Handmade fabrics and vases decorate the halls.

Handgearbeitete Stoffe und Gefäße dekorieren die Hallen.

02 | Beside the pool deck, there are also four whirlpools on the rooftop.

Neben dem Pooldeck gibt es zudem vier Whirlpools auf dem Dach.

03 | The colonial style is formative, interfused with modern design.

Der Kolonialstil ist prägend, durchsetzt mit modernem Design.

04 | For outdoor use: The spa's treatment areas.

Für Anwendungen im Freien: die Behandlungsplätze des Spa.

casa nalum | riviera maya . mexico
DESIGN: Pia Hagerman, Jokin De Luisa

Guests of the Casa Nalum have all the time in the world to sample the many different kinds of relaxation. Privacy is not interrupted by anyone in this house, which only has three rooms. Walls and closed doors are superfluous here. Spacious open surfaces define the view. In the center is the living room with its giant sofa. This is where Western civilization meets Caribbean flair, and not only as far as design is concerned. Guests have the opportunity to watch the latest Hollywood movies on a large screen or simply to enjoy the views over the ocean. Also in the rooms Caribbean architecture merges with modern design. The white four-poster bed of the large room stands under the open wooden beams of the palm covered roof. The respectful use of water is a condition, which the house must adhere to, as it is located inside a biosphere reserve. This does not signify any limitations for the guests however. On the contrary, due to the size of the house the service is completely directed towards individual wishes. So the chef will prepare anything the guests desire and the butler is happy to set the table on the beach or on the rooftop terrace.

Wie viele Facetten Entspannung haben kann, können die Gäste des Casa Nalum in aller Ruhe ausprobieren. Die Privatsphäre wird in diesem lediglich vier Zimmer umfassenden Haus von niemandem gestört. So sind auch Wände und verschlossene Türen überflüssig. Großzügige offene Flächen bestimmen das Bild. Im Zentrum steht das Wohnzimmer mit seinem riesigen Sofa. Hier trifft westliche Zivilisation auf karibisches Flair, nicht nur was das Design angeht. Schließlich hat der Gast die Möglichkeit, sich entweder die neuesten Hollywood-Filme auf einem Großbildschirm anzusehen oder einfach den Blick auf den Ozean zu genießen. Auch in den Zimmern verbindet sich karibische Architektur mit modernem Design. So steht das weiße Himmelbett des größten Zimmers unter den offenen Holzverstrebungen des spitzen, mit Palmenwedeln bedeckten Daches. Der besondere Umgang mit Wasser ist eine Auflage, die das Haus erfüllen muss, da es sich in einem Biosphären Reservat befindet. Für den Gast bedeutet das aber keinerlei Einschränkung. Im Gegenteil, aufgrund der Größe des Hauses richtet sich der Service komplett nach seinen individuellen Wünschen. So bereitet der Koch alles zu, was sich die Gäste wünschen und der Butler deckt den Tisch am Strand genauso wie auf der Dachterrasse.

01 | Sian Kaan–where the sky is born. This is the name of the biosphere reserve, which surrounds the house. The biggest bedroom is also stylishly heavenly.

Sian Kaan - wo der Himmel geboren wurde. So heißt das Biosphären Reservat, das das Haus umgibt. Stilecht himmlisch ist auch das größte Schlafzimmer.

02 | Around three acres of land belongs to Casa Nalum. The best views of the tropical forest and Caribbean ocean can be admired from the rooftop terrace.

Rund ein Hektar Land gehören zum Casa Nalum. Den besten Blick über tropischen Wald und karibisches Meer hat man von der Dachterrasse.

03 | Clear lines and light colors do not just merge in the living room with Caribbean elements like wicker furniture.

Klare Linien und helle Farben verbinden sich nicht nur im Wohnzimmer mit karibischen Elementen, wie geflochtenem Mobiliar.

04 | The lagoon right by the house – a huge private bathtub, which the
guests only have to share with tropical fish.

Die Lagune direkt am Haus – eine überdimensionale private
Badewanne, die die Gäste nur mit tropischen Fischen teilen müssen.

04

05 | Included in the conveniences of the resorts are a personal maid,
butler, chef and gardener.

Zu den Annehmlichkeiten des Resorts gehören ein eigenes
Zimmermädchen, ein Butler, ein Koch und ein Gärtner.

cavas wine lodge | mendoza . argentina

DESIGN: Teresa Giustinian, Felicitas Bermudez, Fernando Malenchini and Diego Gonzalez Pondal (GPM)

The scenic backdrop alone is impressive: the mighty, snow-capped mountains of the Andes, along the foot of which sheer endless vineyards stretch. The lodge is located in arguably the most renowned producing region of Argentina and once used to be a large vineyard. Evidence of this can still be seen in the architecture of the main house: a stately colonial palace with columns, arches and towers. Ambulatories envelop the inner courtyard, trick fountains ripple. A romantic ambience, also for honeymooners, who want to dine here, enjoy wine tasting or simply unwind by the pool. The apartments of the lodge act as contrast in style. They can be found between the rows of over 50 year old vines. From the exterior the bungalows appear to be futuristic forms. Their edges are rounded off and fully coordinated the ascent to the rooftop terrace rises and flows into a chimney with integrated fireplace. The architect's style also dominates in the interior: with individually shaped passages, alcoves in the bare walls and bathrooms with quarrystone walls and polished concrete. Warm tones and a historic touch however are brought in by the furniture and accessories. In such a way that the house connects tradition with modernity—a trademark for the style of the new wine world from overseas. And it's this world which the guests can completely immerse themselves in.

Allein schon die landschaftliche Kulisse beeindruckt: Mächtige, schneebedeckte Berge der Anden, zu dessen Füßen sich schier endlose Weinberge erstrecken. Die Lodge liegt im wohl renommiertesten Anbaugebiet von Argentinien und war selbst einmal ein großes Weingut. Davon zeugt auch noch die Architektur des Haupthauses: ein stattlicher Kolonialpalast mit Säulen, Bögen und Türmen. Arkaden umschließen den Innenhof, Wasserspiele plätschern hier vor sich hin. Ein romantisches Ambiente, auch für Honeymooner, die hier speisen, Weinproben erleben oder einfach am Pool ausspannen wollen. Einen Kontrast im Stil setzen die Apartements der Lodge. Sie befinden sich mitten zwischen den über 50 Jahre alten Rebstöcken. Von außen erscheinen die Bungalows wie futuristische Gebilde. Ihre Kanten sind abgerundet, wie aus einem Guss entsteht der Aufgang zur Dachterrasse und mündet in eine Kaminspitze mit integrierter Feuerstelle. Auch innen dominiert der Stil des Architekten: mit eigenwillig geformten Durchgängen, Nischen in den kahlen Wänden und Bädern aus Bruchsteinwänden und poliertem Beton. Warme Töne und einen historischen Touch bringen indes Möbel und Accessoires hinein. Das Haus verbindet Tradition mit Moderne – Kennzeichen für den Stil der neuen Weinwelt aus Übersee. Und in diese Welt können hier die Gäste ganz und gar eintauchen.

01 | The apartements are furnished in a contemporary hacienda style.

Die Apartements sind in zeitgenössischem Hacienda-Stil eingerichtet.

02 | Living amongst the grapevines in impressive nature scenery.

Wohnen inmitten der Weinstöcke in beeindruckender Naturkulisse.

01 | The topic of wine dominates the new spa.

In dem neuen Spa dominiert das Thema Wein.

patios de cafayate hotel & spa | cafayate . argentina

DESIGN: Laura Garramón and Marcela Rey

The Cafayate Valley is among the most important wine regions in Argentina. It is the northern most producing region in the country and is located 5,100 feet high. In the background the Andes Mountains rise up over 18,000 feet high. Those who go hiking here find bizarre, eroded rock formations. The temperature is pleasant during the day, the nights can, however, be quite cool, which is not only an advantage for the grapevines. The hotel appeals to travelers who wish to explore this world. At one time it was a winery—a proud structure in the Spanish colonial style. The old cellar and the inner courtyards of the hotel, as well as the newly constructed spa, are particularly appealing. The wellness hideaway is presented, in contrast to the main house, in a contemporarily elegant style as a modern tract made of steel and glass in which numerous "vino-therapies" are offered: Grape seed peeling, for example, or applications with grape mash. A heated pool in front of the hotel is very inviting. The 27 rooms and three suites are located directly in the main part of the old winery: Grand guest rooms with the splendor of days gone by. Desks, beds and bureaus are antiques, heavy red drapes frame the widows. Genuine silver is still used in the restaurant. An emphasis is placed here on distinguished style without being cramped—connoisseurs of good wines will be in the right place here.

Das Tal von Cafayate zählt zu den wichtigsten Weinregionen Argentiniens. Es ist das nördlichste Anbaugebiet des Landes und befindet sich auf 1700 Meter Höhe. Im Rücken erheben sich die Anden auf über 6000 Meter. Wer dort wandern geht, stößt auf bizarr erodierte Felsformen. Die Temperaturen am Tag sind angenehm, die Nächte dagegen kühl, was nicht nur ein Vorteil für die Weinreben ist. So wendet sich das Hotel an Reisende, denen es Freude bereitet, in diese Welt einzutauchen. Es war selbst einst ein Weingut – ein stolzer Bau im spanischen Kolonialstil. Glanzstücke sind die alten Keller und Innenhöfe des Hauses, aber auch das neu errichtete Spa. Das Wellness-Refugium präsentiert sich, im Unterschied zum Haupthaus, zeitgenössisch elegant als ein moderner Stahl- und Glastrakt, in dem zahlreiche Vinotherapien angeboten werden: Traubenkern-Peeling etwa oder Anwendungen mit der Traubenmaische. Im Garten vor dem Hotel lockt ein beheizter Pool. Die 27 Zimmer und drei Suiten befinden sich direkt im Hauptteil des alten Gutes: würdevolle Gästezimmer mit dem Glanz einer früheren Zeit. Schreibtische, Betten und Kommoden sind antiquarische Stücke, wuchtige rote Vorhänge umrahmen die Fenster. Im Restaurant wird noch Silberbesteck aufgelegt. Man legt hier Wert auf einen distinguierten Stil ohne zu verkrampfen – für Freunde der guten Tropfen eigentlich genau die richtige Tonlage.

02 | The view is focused on antiques in the rooms.

In den Zimmern richtet sich der Blick auf die antiquarischen Stücke.

03 | The hotel is located in the middle of the vineyards of the winery, El Esteco.

Das Hotel liegt zwischen den Rebstöcken des Weinguts El Esteco.

03

hotel index

hotel index

Country / Location		Address	Information	Architecture & Design	Page
Italy	Gargnano	Grand Hotel a Villa Feltrinelli Via Rimembranza 38-40 25084 Gargnano Italy www.villafeltrinelli.com	opened 2001 21 rooms and suites, boat house with private landing pier, swim-ming pool, library, open fireside, private dining room. Indoor dining room, outdoor dining terrace La Pergola, salon boat La Contessa. Situated on the western shore of the Lake Garda. 80 km from Verona Airport and 140 km from Milano Linate Airport.	Pamela Babey	28
Spain	Mallorca	Son Brull Hotel & Spa Carretera palma-pollenca MA 2200 km 49,8 Mallorca Spain www.sonbrull.com	opened 2003 23 rooms, restaurant, bar, spa, indoor and outdoor pool, tennis court. 2 km from the village center of Pollença. 55 km from the airport.	Ignazi Forteza	32
Greece	Mykonos	Ostraco Suites 846 00 Mykonos Greece www.ostraco.gr	opened 1989, reopened 2005 22 rooms equipped with DVD, mini bar, LCD TV, Hifi. Some suites have indoor or outdoor jacuzzis. The hotel is situated 600 meters from from Mykonos town and 2 km from the airport.	Zannis Koukas Aggelos Aggelopoulos Dimitrios Mantikas	36
Morocco	Skoura	Dar Ahlam Douar Oulad Cheik Ali Skoura (Province d'Ouarzazate) Morocco www.darahlam.com	opened 2002 12 rooms, restaurant, meeting facilities from 5 to 30 people. Beauty center, hamam, jacuzzi, heated pool. Located on the road to Ouarzazate towards Olerzouga (Dades Valley).	Thierry Teyssier	42
Morocco	Marakech	Casa Lalla Riad Zitoun Lakdime 16 Derb Jamaa Marrakech Morocco www.casalalla.com	opened 2003 8 rooms with four standard and four suites, two of them have a fireplace. Restaurant, small pool, hamam and massages. Located in the middle of the city, 3 minutes from Djaama El Fna-Square. 3 km from the airport.	Annabel and Pierre Olivier	46

hotel index

Country / Location		Address	Information	Architecture & Design	Page
Mauritius	Turtle Bay	The Oberoi, Mauritius Turtle Bay, Pointe aux Piments Mauritius www.oberoihotels.com	opened 2000, reopened 2004 72 villas in total including 1 royal villa with private pool, 26 luxury villas—16 of them with private pool—and 45 luxury pavilions. 2 restaurants, 3 bars. 2 swimming pools, Oberoi Spa by Banyan Tree, 2 tennis courts, water sports. 55 minutes drive from Sir Sewoosagar Ramgoolam International Airport.	Lek Bunnag H. L. Lim	50
Namibia	Sossusvlei	Little Kulala P.O. Box 5219 3 Autumn Street Rivonia 2128 South Africa www.wilderness-safaris.com	opened 2002, reopened 2006 11 chalets, each has its own plunge pool and a swimming pool. Lounge, bar, dining room, library, wine cellar, craft boutique and veranda. Located east of the Namibian desert. 1 hour flight and 5 hour drive (350 km) from Windhoek.	Laurie Owen Andy Chase	56
South Africa	Kruger National Park	Singita Sweni Lodge Sweni River South Africa www.singita.com	opened 2005 6 suiten, restaurant, wine cellar, swimming pool, gym and bush spa, skin care treatments, massage treatments. 90 minutes flight from Johannesburg to Satara airstrip and from there a 40 minutes drive to the lodge.	Boyd Ferguson, Cecile and Boyd Andrew Makin, OM Design Workshop	60
South Africa	Greater Kruger Area	Royal Malewane P.O. Box 1542, Hoedspruit, 1380 South Africa www.royalmalewane.com	6 luxury suites with deck and private plunge pools and fireplace. Royal and Malewane Suites (210 m²) for 4 guests in 2 en-suite rooms with private lounge, dining facilities, pool, private butler, chef and private game drives. Dining area, library, gym and bush spa. 50 km from Hoedspruit.	Ralph Krall, Phil and Liz Biden	64
South Africa	Marakele National Park	Marataba The Waterberg Limpopo Province South Africa www.marataba.com	15 luxury tented suites with stone bathrooms, underfloor heating outdoor showers, restaurant. Located within its private 23,000 hectares concession in the Marakele National Park of the Limpopo Province. 3 hours drive or 50 minutes by air from Johannesburg. Jill Hunter, Jacqui Hunter,	Nicholas Plewman & Hunter Family	68

hotel index

Country / Location		Address	Information	Architecture & Design	Page
South Africa	Swellendam	Bloomestate 276 Voortrekstreet P.O. Box 672 Swellendam 6740 South Africa www.bloomestate.com	opened 2003 7 rooms, guest lounge, bar, terrace, heated pool, open air jacuzzi, natural pond. Design furniture, WLAN, DVD and i-pod music station in each room. Wellness treatments. Around 2 hours drive from Cape Town.	Joke Hensema	72
South Africa	Hermanus-Gansbaai	Grootbos Hermanus-Gansbaai South Africa www.grootbos.com	garden lodge opened 1995, forest lodge 2005 26 suites with balcony, lounge and separate bedroom, airy bathroom, restaurant, bar. Situated 30 km southeast of Hermanus in the Walker Bay.	Vaughan Russell Eloise Collocott-Russell Dorothé Lutzeyer	76
South Africa	Plettenberg	Tsala Treetop Lodge Plettenberg Bay South Africa www.tsala.co.za	opened 2001 10 suites with private plunge pool, sun deck fireplace, wooden elevated walkways between suites and main complex. Situated between Knysna and Plettenberg Bay, 5 hours from Cape Town, small airport at Knysna and Plettenberg Bay.	Bruce Stafford and Hunter Family	82
India	Udaipur	Taj Lake Palace P.O. Box No. 5 Pichola Lake Udaipur 313 001 Rajasthan, India www.tajhotels.com	Reopened 2000 83 rooms und 17 suites. Restaurants, pool, spa. Historic building from 1746. Located on an island in Lake Pichola. 26 km from the airport and 1 km from the city center.	James Park Associates	86
Sri Lanka	Galle	Lighthouse Hotel & Spa Dadella, Galle Sri Lanka www.lighthousehotel- andspa.com	opened 1996 63 rooms, Cardamom Café, Anchor Bar & Grill, pool side bar. Adam & Eve Spa Dining. Spa, 2 swimming pools, gym, squash, tennis, table tennis, library, yoga, excursions to rain forests. 146 km from the International airport and 12 km from the domestic airport.	Geoffrey Bawa	90

hotel index

hotel index

Country / Location		Address	Information	Architecture & Design	Page
French Polynesia	Bora Bora	St. Regis Resort Bora Bora Motu Ome'e BP 506 Bora Bora, 98730 French Polynesia www.stregis.com/borabora	opened 2006 100 luxury over-water and beach villas, many with terrace whirl-pools or private swimming pools. Restaurant, private swim-up bar, private lagoonarium, nanny service. Arrive by ferry or in Bora Bora at Motu Mute Airport; also with private yacht, jet or helicopter.	Pierre Lacombe Miriam Hall	114
Fiji	Vatulele Island	Vatulele Island Resort Vatulele Island Fiji http://www.vatulele.com	opened 1990 19 villas. Dive school, 22 dive sites nearby. A 30 minutes flight by seaplane from Nadi International Airport	Martin Livingston Doug Nelson Henry Crawford	118
Connecticut	Washington	Mayflower Inn & Spa 118 Woodbury Road Route 47 Washington CT 06793 USA www.mayflowerinn.com	opened 1992 30 rooms and suites. Restaurant: classic American, tap room, spa dining. Spa, indoor and outdoor pools, tennis, gardens, labyrinth. 10 miles from Oxford Private Airport, 35 miles from Hartford International, 80 miles from JFK.	Randall Ridless	122
Massachusetts	Lenox	Wheatleigh Hawthorne Road Lenox MA 01240 USA http://www.wheatleigh.com	reopened 2000 9 suites, 100 rooms. Outdor heated pool, tennis court, boccia ball field, bikes for guests available. Restaurants. 3 hours to New York and 2 hours to Boston.	Calvin Tsao Zack McKown	126
Turks and Caicos	Providenciales	Amanyara Northwest Point Providenciales Turks and Caicos Islands British West Indies www.amanresorts.com	opened 2006 40 pavilions, restaurant, bar, beach club, swimming pools, library, boutique, screening-room, fitness centre, tennis courts. Located along the coast of Northwest Point, adjacent to Malcolm's Beach on Providenciales. 25 minutes from International Airport on Providenciales.	Team around Jean Michel Gathy	132

hotel index

Country / Location		Address	Information	Architecture & Design	Page
Puerto Rico	Vieques	Hix Island House HC-02 Box 14902 Vieques Puerto Rico 00765 www.hixislandhouse.com	opened 1986 13 rooms, pool, fully equipped lofts with kitchens stocked for breakfast, yoga and massage, outdoor showers. 6 km from the airport	John Hix	138
Dominican Republic	Puerto Plata	Casa Colonial Playa Dorado, Puerto Plata Dominican Republic www.ehbox.com	opened 2004 50 rooms, Restaurant Lucia (dinner only) and Restaurant Veranda (breakfast and lunch). 20 minutes from Puerto Plata International Airport.	Sarah Garcia	142
Mexico	Riviera Maya	Casa Nalum Carretera Tulum-Boca Paila Sian Ka'an Biosphere Reserve Quintana Roo, Mexico www.nalum.com	opened 2005 4 bedrooms, 2 en-suite bathrooms, all-inclusive holidays: airport transfers, 3 meals a day, drinks, massages, excursions, butler service. Inside the biosphere reserve of Sian Ka'an, Unesco World Heritage site. (120 km) 2 hours drive from Cancun International Airport.	Pia Hagerman Jokin De Luisa	146
Argentina	Mendoza	Cavas Wine Lodge Costaflores s/n Alto Agrelo M 5507, Mendoza Argentina www.cavaswinelodge.com	opened 2005 14 rooms (vignettes), restaurant, spa with wine therapy treatments, pool, gym, cellar with the best Argentine labels. 35 km from the airport.	Teresa Giustinian, Felicitas Bermudez, Fernando Malenchini and Diego Gonzalez Pondal (GPM)	152
Argentina	Cafayate	Patios de Cafayate Hotel & Spa Ruta Nacional 40 y 68 Cafayate, Salta 4427 Argentina www.spghoneymoons.com	opened 2005 27 rooms and 3 suites with vineyard and garden view. Restaurant, outside swimming pool, wine spa, art function room, reading room. 3 hours from Salta Airport (186 km).	Laura Garramón, Marcela Rey	156

architects & designers

photo credits

all other photos by Roland Bauer and Martin Nicholas Kunz

imprint

Bibliographic information published by Die Deutsche Bibliothek. Die Deutsche Bibliothek lists this publication in the Deutsche Nationalbibliografie; detailed bibliographic data are available on the internet at http://ddb.de
ISBN 10: 3-89986-075-6
ISBN 13: 978-3-89986-075-7

1st edition

Printed in Austria
by Vorarlberger Verlagsanstalt AG, Dornbirn

Editors | Martin Nicholas Kunz, Hanna Martin
Editorial coordination | Rosina Geiger, Hanna Martin, Anne-Kathrin Meier
Copy editing | Christiane Niemann, Despina Vradelis
Translations | C.E.T. Central European Translations, Claudia Ade Team, Stuttgart

Layout | Jasmina Bremer
Imaging | Jan Hausberg

avedition GmbH
Königsallee 57 | 71638 Ludwigsburg | Germany
p +49-7141-1477391 | f +49-7141-1477399
www.avedition.com | contact@avedition.com

Further information and links at
www.bestdesigned.com
www.fusion-publishing.com

Texts (pages) | Anna Streubert (editorial, 12, 72, 102), riva-medien (8, 16, 20, 24, 28, 32, 36, 56, 76, 90), Carolin Schöngarth (46, 118, 122, 132, 138, 146), Heinfried Tacke (50, 60, 68, 82, 86, 94, 98, 106, 114, 126, 142, 152, 156), Bettina Winterfeld (42), all other texts by fusion publishing.

Special thanks to Stella Andronikou, Ostraco Suites | Florencia Arenaza, Patios de Cafayate Hotel & Spa | Kirsten Beck, Kleber PR Network | Ulrike Birner, ArabellaSheraton | Chiara Bocchini, Charming House DD.724 | Cecilia, Cavas Wine Lodge | Karen Costes, Bourg Tibourg | Henry Crawford, Vatulele Island Resort | Scott Crouch, Wilde & Partner | Miguel Cunat, Sri Lanka In Style | Bettina Faust, LueersPartner Public Relations GmbH | Michael Franco, Hix Island House | Martina Frühe , ZFL PRCo | Sanjiva Gautamadasa, Jetwing | Bob Gevinski, Bob Gevinski Photography | Lisa Hedley, Hedley Media | Roland Hoede, Exclusive Travel Choice | Claudia Hubberten, Son Brull Hotel & Spa | Ian Hunter, Hunter Hotels | Ingo Jacob, Travel Consultants Africa | Merehani Jithame, St. Regis Resort Bora Bora | Barbara Lueers, LueersPartner Public Relations GmbH | Nimalka Morahella, Sri Lanka In Style | Feyza Morgül, Uschi Liebl PR | Stéphanie Moulin, Lever de Rideau | Rejane Narbonnet, St. Regis Resort Bora Bora | Anjali Nihalchand, Amanresorts | Elise O'Connell, The Grove | Markus Odermatt, Grand Hotel a Villa Feltrinelli | Annabel Olivier, Casa Lalla | Fernando Peña, Victoria Hotels & Resorts | Leana Pieris, Taru Villas Taprobana | Richard Plattner, Hotel Castell | Frauke Rothschuh, Text & Aktion | Helen Schröger, Schaffelhuber Communications | Mark Selwood, Chateau de la Couronne | Roberto Sidoti, Casa Nalum | Carmen Stromberger, ZFL PRCo | Putu A. Susenayasa, Alila Hotels and Resorts Bali | Carla van der Ven, Bloomestate | Kathy Wayland, Royal Malewane | Marc Wilhelm, Wheatleigh | Avon Wong, Amanresorts | Magdalena Wozniak, STR Destination for their support.

Martin Nicholas Kunz
1957 born in Hollywood. Founder of fusion publishing creating content for architecture, design, travel, and lifestyle publications.

Hanna Martin
1979 born in Freiburg. Well-travelled editorial manager for several hotel and architecture books. She studied audiovisual media with a main focus on design.

best designed:
ecological hotels
affordable hotels
modular houses
outdoor living
hotel pools

best designed hotels:
asia pacific
americas
europe I (urban)
europe II (countryside)

best designed wellness hotels:
asia pacific
americas
europe
africa & middle east

All books are released in German and English